CANTERBURY STUDIES IN ANGLICANISM
Worship-Shaped Life

CANTERBURY STUDIES
IN ANGLICANISM

Series Editors: Martyn Percy and Ian Markham

Worship-Shaped Life

Liturgical Formation and the People of God

Edited by
Ruth Meyers and Paul Gibson

Morehouse Publishing

CANTERBURY
PRESS
Norwich

© The Contributors 2010

First published in 2010 by the Canterbury Press Norwich
Editorial office
13–17 Long Lane,
London, EC1A 9PN, UK

Canterbury Press is an imprint of Hymns Ancient and Modern Ltd
(a registered charity)
St Mary's Works, St Mary's Plain,
Norwich, NR3 3BH, UK

www.scm-canterburypress.co.uk

First published in North America in 2010 by
Morehouse Publishing, 4775 Linglestown Road,
Harrisburg, PA 17112
Morehouse Publishing, 445 Fifth Avenue, New York, NY 10016
Morehouse Publishing is an imprint of
Church Publishing Incorporated.
www.morehousepublishing.org

British Library Cataloguing in Publication data

A catalogue record for this book is available
from the British Library

978 1 84825 007 9

Typeset by Manila Typesetting Company
Printed and bound in Great Britain by
CPI Antony Rowe, Chippenham, SN14 6LH

CONTENTS

v

FOREWORD TO THE SERIES

by the Archbishop of Canterbury

The question 'What is the real identity of Anglicanism?' has become more pressing and more complex than ever before in the last
decade or so, ecumenically as well as internally. Is the Anglican
identity a matter of firm Reformed or Calvinist principle, resting
its authoritative appeal on a conviction about the sovereignty
and all-sufficiency of Scripture interpreted literally? Is it a form
of non-papal Catholicism, strongly focused on sacramental and
ministerial continuity, valuing the heritage not only of primitive
Christianity but also of mediaeval and even post-Reformation
Catholic practice and devotion? Is it an essentially indeterminate
Christian culture, particularly well-adapted to the diversity of
national and local sympathies and habits? Is the whole idea of
an 'ism' misplaced here?

Each of these models has its defenders across the Communion;
and each has some pretty immediate consequences for the polity
and politics of the global Anglican family. Some long for a much
more elaborately confessional model than has generally been the
case – the sort of model that those who defined the boundaries of
the Church of England in the sixteenth century were very wary
of. Some are happy with the idea of the Communion becoming
a federation of local bodies with perhaps, in the long run, quite
markedly diverging theologies and disciplines. The disagree-
ments over the ordination of women and the Church's response
to lesbian and gay people have raised basic issues around the
liberty of local churches to decide what are thought by many to
be secondary matters; the problem then being that not everyone

agrees that they are secondary. The question of identity is inseparable from the question of unity: to recognize another community as essentially the same, whatever divergences there may be
in language and practice, is necessary for any unity that is more
than formal – for a unity that issues in vigorous evangelism and
consistent 'diaconal' service to the world.

And this means in turn that questions about Anglican identity
will inevitably become questions about the very nature of the
Church – and thus the nature of revelation and incarnation and
the character of God's activity. I believe it is generally a piece of
deplorably overheated rhetoric to describe those holding different views around the kind of questions I have mentioned as being
adherents of 'different religions'; but there is an uncomfortable
sense in which this exaggeration reminds us that the line between
primary and secondary issues is not self-evidently clear – or at
least that what we say about apparently secondary matters may
reveal something about our primary commitments.

The long and short of it is that we should be cautious of saying
of this or that development or practice 'It isn't Anglican', as if
that settled the matter. One of the first tasks we need to pursue
in the current climate is simply to look at what Anglicans say
and do. We need to watch Anglicans worshipping, constructing
patterns for decision-making and administration, arguing over a
variety of moral issues (not only sexuality), engaging in spiritual
direction and the practices of private prayer. Without this, we
shan't be in a good position to assess whether it's the same religion; and we are very likely to be assuming that what we take for
granted is the norm for a whole church or family of churches.

The books in this series are attempts to do some of this 'watching' – not approaching the question of identity in the abstract
but trying to discern how Anglicans identify themselves in their
actual life together, locally and globally. I'd like to think that
they might challenge some of the more unhelpful clichés that can
be thrown around in debate, the stereotypes used by both Global
South and Global North about each other. If it is true that – as I
have sometimes argued in other places – true interfaith dialogue
only begins as you watch the other when their faces are turned

to God, this must be true a fortiori in the Christian context. And I hope that some of these essays will allow a bit of that sort of watching. If they do, they will have helped us turn away from the lethal temptation to talk always about others when our backs are turned to them (and to God).

We all know that simply mapping the plurality of what Anglicans do is not going to answer the basic question, of course. But it is a necessary discipline for our spiritual health. It is in the light of this that we can begin to think through the broader theological issues. Let's say for the sake of argument that church communities in diverse contexts with diverse convictions about some of the major issues of the day do as a matter of bare fact manage to acknowledge each other as Anglican disciples of Jesus Christ to the extent that they are able to share some resources in theological training and diaconal service: the task then is to try and tease out what – as a matter of bare fact – makes them recognizable to each other. Not yet quite theology, but a move towards it, and above all a move away from mythologies and projections.

If I had to sum up some of my own convictions about Anglican identity, I should, I think, have to begin with the fact that, at the beginning of the English Reformation, there was a widespread agreement that Catholic unity was secured not by any external structures alone but by the faithful ministration of Word and Sacrament – 'faithful' in the sense of unadulterated by mediaeval agendas about supernatural priestly power or by the freedom of a hierarchical Church to add new doctrinal refinements to the deposit of faith. Yet as this evolved a little further, the Reformers in Britain turned away from a second-generation Calvinism which would have alarmed Calvin himself and which argued for a wholly literal application of biblical law to the present times and the exclusion from church practice of anything not contained in the plain words of Scripture. Gradually the significance of a continuous ministry in the historic style came more into focus as a vehicle of mutual recognition, eventually becoming the straightforward appeal to apostolic episcopal succession often thought to be a central characteristic of the Anglican tradition.

The blend of concern for ordered ministry (and thus ordered worship), freedom from an uncritical affirmation of hierarchical ecclesiastical authority, with the appeal to Scripture at the heart of this, and the rooted belief that the forms of common worship were the most important clues about what was held to be recognizably orthodox teaching – this blend or fusion came to define the Anglican ethos in a growing diversity of cultural contexts. Catholic, yes, in the sense of seeing the Church today as responsible to its history and to the gifts of God in the past, even those gifts given to people who have to be seen as in some ways in error. Reformed, yes, in the sense that the principle remains of subjecting the state of the Church at any given moment to the judgement of Scripture – though not necessarily therefore imagining that Scripture alone offers the answer to every contemporary question. And running through the treatment of these issues, a further assumption that renewal in Christ does not abolish but fulfils the long-frustrated capacities of human beings: that we are set free to sense and to think the texture of God's Wisdom in the whole of creation and at the same time to see how it is itself brought to fulfilment in the cross of Jesus.

This is the kind of definition that a sympathetic reading of the first two Anglican centuries might suggest. It certainly has implications for where we find the centre for such a definition in our own day. But the point is that it is a historical argument, not one from first principles; or rather, the principles emerge as the history is traced. Once again, it is about careful watching – not as an excuse for failing to look for a real theological centre but as a discipline of discerning the gifts that have actually been given to us as Anglicans.

Not many, I suspect, would seriously want to argue that the Anglican identity can be talked about without reference to Catholic creeds and ministry, or to think that a 'family' of churches can be spoken of without spelling out at least the essential family resemblances in terms of what Christ has uniquely done and what Christ continues to do in his Body through Word and Sacrament. But to understand how this does and does not, can and cannot, work, we need the kind of exact and imaginative study that this series offers us. I hope that many readers will take the trouble to work with the grain of such investigations, so that our life in the Communion (and in communion itself in its fullest sense, the communion of the Holy Spirit) will be enriched as well as calmed, and challenged as well as reinforced.

+*Rowan Cantuar:*
from Lambeth Palace, Advent 2009

ABOUT THE CONTRIBUTORS

The Rt Revd Solomon Amusan, MLitt, DMin, was the Registrar and senior lecturer of liturgy at Vining College of Theology, Akure, and later at Immanuel College of Theology, Ibadan, both in Nigeria, before he was appointed the Provost of the Cathedral Church of St Peter, Aremo, Ibadan, from where he was elected the Bishop of Oke-Ogun Diocese, Church of Nigeria, Anglican Communion.

The Revd Canon Cynthia Botha is the Co-ordinating Secretary of the Publishing Committee and Convenor of the Liturgical Committee for the Anglican Church of Southern Africa. She also serves as the Liaison Officer for Liturgy for the Anglican Communion.

Dr Carol Doran, DMA, is an independent scholar and teacher who has held tenured faculty positions at The Virginia Theological Seminary in Alexandria, Virginia, and at Bexley Hall in Rochester, New York, USA. Her work is currently centred in developing Project Shepherd's Voice, a programme that enables clergy to work with music and musicians to build congregations.

The Revd Mark Earey is Tutor in Liturgy and Co-Director of the Centre for Ministerial Formation at the Queen's Foundation for Ecumenical Theological Education, Birmingham, UK.

The Revd Paul Gibson, now retired, served as Liturgical Officer of the Anglican Church of Canada and as Co-ordinator for Liturgy for the Anglican Consultative Council.

ABOUT THE CONTRIBUTORS

The Revd Dr Richard Geoffrey Leggett is Associate Dean and Professor of Liturgical Studies at Vancouver School of Theology, Vancouver, Canada.

The Revd Tomas S. Maddela, STD, is Professor of Liturgics at St Andrew's Theological Seminary, and Lecturer at the Asian Institute for Liturgy and Music and at the Maryhill School of Theology, all located in Quezon City, Philippines.

The Revd Dr Ruth A. Meyers is Hodges-Haynes Professor of Liturgics at Church Divinity School of the Pacific, Berkeley, California, USA.

The Revd Dr Juan M. C. Oliver was Adjunct Professor of Liturgics and Director of the Hispanic/Latino programme in Theology and Pastoral Ministry at the General Theological Seminary, New York, USA, until his retirement in 2008.

INTRODUCTION

For the past half century, many provinces of the Anglican Communion have engaged in a process of liturgical renewal and revision. An important factor in this renewal was the grassroots liturgical movement of the mid twentieth century, fostered in part by organizations such as Parish and People in the Church of England and Associated Parishes for Liturgy and Mission in the Episcopal Church (USA) and the Anglican Church of Canada. Emphasizing a Pauline theology of the Church as the Body of Christ, leaders of the liturgical movement urged changes in worship practices in order to renew and strengthen the church's witness in the world. A renewed liturgy would enable more effective formation of the people of God, the members of Christ's Body. Nourished by the Body of Christ received in the Eucharist, members of that Body would go forth from those celebrations to be the Body of Christ in the world.

As the liturgical movement gathered steam in various churches of the Anglican Communion, its leaders began to recognize the limitations of the Book of Common Prayer. The structures and texts of the various books in use around the communion were largely unchanged from the forms introduced during the sixteenth and seventeenth centuries. Liturgical and biblical scholarship in the twentieth century, undertaken by scholars from various Christian traditions, was introducing new understandings of the worship of the church in its earliest centuries, a period that Anglicans have considered as offering important norms for worship. Gradually, the emphasis of the liturgical movement shifted from the reform of worship practices to the revision of liturgical texts. The 1958 Lambeth Conference, acknowledging work on prayer book revision in various provinces of the communion, recognized that the 1662 Book of Common Prayer was no longer the guiding standard for Anglican worship.

Those provinces which have undertaken prayer book revision have been able to utilize the insights of recent liturgical scholarship and to develop prayer books that are better suited to their particular cultural contexts. Over the past three decades, the work of the International Anglican Liturgical Consultation has both affirmed revisions already completed and offered guidance for provinces engaged in revision of their worship books. The appendix to this volume, 'A Short History of the International Anglican Liturgical Consultation', tells the story of this work and lists the publications arising from its meetings.

Yet the revision of texts and rites has not by itself accomplished the renewal that was the guiding vision of the liturgical movement. In 2003, participants in the International Anglican Liturgical Consultation gathered for a conference on the subject of liturgical formation, seeking to understand the various challenges and possibilities in the provinces of the Anglican Communion. The contributions in this volume were originally presented at that meeting; some of the authors have revised their chapters for this publication.

As several of the chapters indicate, 'liturgical formation' has various meanings and implications. Mark Earey proposes that these meanings include formation *for* liturgy, that is, deepening understanding through education; formation *for those who lead liturgy*, which is sometimes referred to as 'training'; and *the way in which liturgy forms* the people of God. The authors of these chapters offer different perspectives on these aspects of liturgical formation.

Tomas Maddela gives particular attention to the liturgical formation of ordinands, while Richard Leggett considers continuing liturgical education for ordained and lay leaders. Both Maddela and Leggett touch on all three aspects that Earey identifies. Those who lead the church's worship must receive not only education about matters such as the historical development of Christian worship, its theology, the structure and content of individual rites, and the pastoral dimensions. They must also receive training in the leadership of public worship and in the crafting of worship services. Moreover, ordinands as well as lay and clergy leaders, like the whole people of God, are themselves formed by worship.

Education and training must continue, Leggett reminds us. Carol Doran, in her chapter on the role of music in liturgical formation, urges that musicians be included among those who receive continuing liturgical education, and that clergy receive continuing education in music. Several of the authors point out that revision of a prayer book or hymnal may be a time when many are receptive to liturgical education, as, for example, Mark Earey experienced in the introduction of *Common Worship* in England. The lack of liturgical education can also be a hindrance to more thorough-going liturgical revision, as Solomon Amusan notes of his experience in Nigeria.

While most of the authors comment on formation *for* worship, all of them also give attention to formation *by* worship. Worship, says Juan Oliver, 'forms the whole person, attitudinally and not only intellectually, by rehearsing our selves, our souls, our bodies through verbal and nonverbal means, engaging us in a semblance of the Reign of God'. Worship engages us in symbolic action that is – or ought to be – characteristic of the Reign of God. Therein, says Oliver, lies a major challenge for those who craft worship. The same symbolic action that can form us for the Reign of God can also deform us, if it is not both attentive to history *and* to the local time, place, and culture.

Other chapters in this collection also call attention to the need to inculturate worship. Carol Doran takes up the question of culture from the perspective of music. Because the phenomenon of music is trans-cultural, it can communicate across cultures, fostering the development of community and even reconciliation, and serving as a vehicle of revelation, as people through music become aware of the presence of God. Richard Leggett calls attention to the importance of inculturation in every context. Too often, he says, those in the dominant or majority culture consider inculturation to be an aspect of ministry to other (minority) racial or ethnic communities and not as a dynamic process at work within the majority culture as well. Solomon Amusan takes his readers to his home of Nigeria, and to the Yoruba tribe. Describing the religious sensibilities and ritual practices of this tribe, Amusan gently criticizes the denial of the Yoruba people's religious sensibilities and the suppression of indigenous religious practices by nineteenth-century missionaries from England. Amusan concludes his chapter by suggesting possibilities for future liturgical revision in the Church of Nigeria, whether by incorporating traditional African elements into the existing liturgies inherited from the Church of England, or by creating a wholly new African liturgical expression.

Ruth Meyers' chapter considers another aspect of the context of worship. Drawing from studies of human development and faith development, she considers the place of children, teens, and young adults in worship and urges their full participation in the liturgical assembly.

Each of these chapters underscores the power of worship to shape the people of God as a people in mission. Each chapter also calls for education and training, not only for those who lead worship but for every member of the assembly. We hope that the vision of these authors and their passion for worship-shaped life will encourage and inspire you, whatever your role in the liturgical assembly.

Ruth A. Meyers and Paul Gibson
All Saints' Day 2009

I

WORSHIP, FORMING AND DEFORMING

Juan M. C. Oliver

I am much honoured to be asked to share with you some thoughts on liturgical formation and how we may engage it today. I will first look at the term liturgical formation and its development, exploring how worship is much more than a vehicle for theological ideas. I will then describe how worship itself forms – and sometimes deforms – Christians, and the importance of personal reflection upon our experience of worship. Finally, I will share some thoughts on intellectual ideas and their role in the liturgical formation of laity and clergy alike.

Liturgical formation

When I was growing up as a Roman Catholic boy in Puerto Rico in the 1950s, I would from time to time hear about 'the formation of seminarians'. This was meant to imply that seminarians had to be 'shaped' – developed into priests in the seminary hothouse through a process of study, work, and guided spiritual development. The term used to convey much more than the secular term 'education', and it denoted a complex process through which the seminarian's sense of self, his skills, and his spiritual life were all in a process of development and growth.

Imagine my surprise when in 1987, during a meeting on the development of the catechumenate in the Episcopal Church, several people began to talk about 'Christian formation' as something different in kind from 'Christian education'.[1] We wanted to drive home the message that what goes on in most Christian education programmes does not take into consideration the development of the whole person. This came in part as a reaction to some Christian educators who insisted that the preparation of Christians for baptism should have a syllabus, lesson plans, even tests, when others insisted that persons exploring the meaning of the Christian experience needed a more holistic process characterized by reflection upon one's life experience in the light of Scripture and the sacraments.

Thus, by employing the term 'Christian formation' we wanted to denote much more than education, pointing to the development of the whole person: head and heart, intellect, will, imagination and emotions; actions as well as thoughts. This led us to the connection between Christian formation and ethics, and therefore to the recovery of the idea of conversion as a process of changing patterns in *behaviour* and not only a change in *ideas*.

At the same time, we were finding that abstract explanations of our creeds and teachings did not satisfy the serious seeker; people wanted deeply to be accompanied along this path of changing behavior, this gradual turning to God and a new way of living, and it seemed to us that pastoral skills such as empathetic listening were more conducive to conversion than lectures on Henry VIII's divorce.

Thus Christian formation as a process distinct from Christian education was born of our concern with the process by which a person is made into a Christian by the Holy Spirit. With Tertullian, we acknowledged that in our post-Christian age, Christians are not born, but made by God in the context of a supportive worshipping assembly.[2] We therefore thought it important to dedicate time, energy, and funds to finding out more about how God makes Christians.

'Christians are made, not born.' Tertullian's statement of course comes as no surprise to theologians. And I dare say that most of us would accurately say that from the point of view of liturgical theology, a Christian is made by taking a holy bath and eating at a holy table with other Christians. I believe this to be profoundly true.

The developmental question, however, still remains: granted that Christians are made through the combined liturgical rites of baptism and Eucharist, how do Christians grow and develop before and after these? And that brings us to the central question of this presentation: What is the relationship between worship and the growth and development of persons into mature Christians?

To be sure, worship alone is not enough to make a mature Christian. When engaged by itself worship can end up being a pharisaical enterprise, art for art's sake, an exquisite idolatry worshipping liturgy instead of God. This is particularly true when worship is divorced from reflection upon Scripture, personal prayer, and the needs of the world. But even if we assume a living worship connected to individual and communal reflection on Scripture, personal prayer, and witness in the world on behalf of the poor and oppressed, the question remains: *How* does worship support us and form us as we grow into our full maturity in Christ?[3]

Worship expresses and gives rise to theological ideas

Most people today, even most liturgical theologians, I dare say, approach worship as a vehicle or container that expresses, conveys, or makes present pre-existing theological meanings. In this view, liturgy is the form; theology is its content. At its best, this view understands worship as a rhetorical means for the communication of religious insights. At worst, this view considers liturgy as rhetorical frosting on the theological cake. In the view of Catherine Bell, a contemporary student of ritual, this view, proposed by the Cambridge School of anthropologists a century

3

ago, did a great disservice to our understanding of ritual, for it
disguised how ritual in fact does much more than *communicate*
ideas. Instead, Bell and others suggest that ritual can in fact *give
rise* to ideas. The traffic moves in both directions. This becomes
more evident as we consider what ritual does to our participating bodies and not only our minds.[4]

> By abstracting the act [of ritual] from its . . . situation and re-
> ducing its convoluted strategies to a set of reversible structures,
> theoretical analysis misses the real dynamics of practice.[5]

If ritual does not merely present pre-existing ideas, what is it that
ritual does? What are its dynamics of practice? I have suggested
elsewhere that ritual forms us by engaging us in a *semblance*
or rehearsal of life as lived in a world different from our everyday world.[6] For Christian worship, whether we call it common
prayer, corporate worship, or liturgy, this 'other world' consists
of life as it would be lived in the presence of God. Our shorthand
for this other world varies; in the Gospels, it is called 'the Kingdom'; in the Syrian tradition, 'the New World'[7]; today we often
refer to it in English as 'the Reign of God'.

Whatever we call it, that world is different from our everyday
life in that it is lived before and with God. We expect it to ar-
rive one day here among us, as we pray in the Lord's Prayer – a
time, we trust, when God will be revealed as all in all. This is a
world characterized by justice, love, compassion, righteousness,
and joy.

Worship engages us in a semblance of this New World and
rehearses us in living this life again and again by practising the
postures, thoughts, attitudes, and feelings of this New World,
learning to live in it so we can welcome its arrival. Thus the liturgical action engages the whole person – not only our thoughts
but our bodies, and our attitudes and feelings as well. Before we
go on to explore the characteristics of Christian ritual, however,
we need to ask further, *How* does worship do this?

I suggest that, briefly put, worship forms the whole person
through a mimetic process of behaving 'as if'. An example might

be helpful. If we attend a performance of Euripides' play *Medea*, and if the actors are even minimally able to act, we will soon forget that they are actors and begin to see and hear Medea, Creon, and the other members of that very dysfunctional family. Thanks to our willing suspension of disbelief – our willingness to 'bracket' our awareness that these are simply actors acting – we can enter into Medea's world and psyche, raging with her in her jealousy, bitterly bringing revenge upon her husband Jason and his paramour Creusa, and horribly killing her sons to spite Jason. We are there, even though, of course, we are not there at all, but in a darkened room in the West End.

In sum, in the liturgical re-presentation of the Reign of God, we enter into that 'as if' experience through the suspension of *dis*belief. As we participate in the semblance of the Reign, the experience rehearses our bodies, imaginations, wills, feelings, and minds in new ways of being an individual and communal body characterized by compassion, justice, and joy – as long as we willingly give ourselves over to the experience. If you wish, you can read this as a contemporary re-statement of the ancient belief that our worship is an exemplar of the eternal liturgy in heaven. As the author of Hebrews puts it:

> For you have not come to the mountain that may be touched and that burned with fire, and to blackness and darkness and tempest, and the sound of a trumpet and the voice of words, so that those who heard it begged that the word should not be spoken to them anymore . . . But you have come to Mount Zion and to the city of the living God, the heavenly Jerusalem, to an innumerable company of angels, to the general assembly and church of the firstborn who are registered in heaven, to God the Judge of all, to the spirits of just men made perfect, to Jesus the Mediator of the new covenant, and to the blood of sprinkling that speaks better things than that of Abel.[8]

Of course, we are not on Mount Zion at all, but, let's say, in London or New York.

In order to articulate further how ritual accomplishes this, Catherine Bell availed herself of the work of the French critic Pierre Bourdieu,[9] who had examined earlier how human beings develop patterns of attitude – both thinking and feeling – out of practising a particular behaviour in an embodied way. Bell applies to ritual Bourdieu's four characteristics of attitude development or *habitus*, 'the principle by which individual and collective practices are produced and the matrix in which objective structures are realized within the (subjective) dispositions that produce practices'.[10] Bourdieu suggested that the body must be studied as the place where the *habitus* makes meaning. His conception of the body is much broader than what we would find in anatomy or physiology; it includes 'the socially informed body with its tastes and distastes, its compulsions and revulsions, with, in a word, all its senses',[11] including, as Bell points out, the sense of ritual.

First, following Bell, ritual practice is situational. It cannot be grasped theoretically outside the situation and place where it takes place. So, for example, the history of liturgical practice cannot be studied properly by examining only texts, without reference to the history of church architecture and ceremonial. When abstracted from them as the history of the development of ideas or meanings about or communicated through liturgy, we are no longer talking about the history of the liturgical *practice* but about the history of *ideas* about it.

Second, ritual practice is strategic, manipulative, and expedient. The practice of ritual in a given place remains always close to the implicit and rudimentary, 'a ceaseless play of situationally effective schemes, tactics, and strategies'.[12] It takes place in a given place, not by application of theories but in an *ad hoc* manner, improvisationally, regardless of how regulated the improvisation is. Worship therefore needs to be studied with an eye to how it facilitates or impedes its strategies, manipulations, and expediencies, all of which point to some sort of desired outcome: the creation of a semblance of the Reign of God.

Third, worship is embedded in a ' "misrecognition" of what it is doing . . . of its limits and constraints, and of the relationship between its ends and its means'.[13] Thus worship is usually blind to the ways in which it actively creates what it seems to be responding to:

> [Ritualization] is a way of acting that sees itself as *responding* to a place, force, problem or tradition. It tends to see itself as the natural or appropriate thing to do in the circumstances. Ritualization does not see how it actively creates place, force, event and tradition; how it redefines or generates the circumstances to which it is responding. It does not see how its own actions reorder and reinterpret the circumstances so as to afford the sense of fit among the many spheres of experience – body, community, and cosmos.[14]

Worship, therefore, presents itself as a response to God's initiative, even though it is something we have crafted 'as the natural or appropriate thing to do in the circumstances' without calling attention to how it is created or 'how it redefines or generates the circumstances to which it is responding'. It does not explain *in practice* how it reorders and reinterprets circumstances in order to bring together coherently the body, community, and cosmos.

Finally, a fourth characteristic of worship is the production of a strategic vision of the order of power in the world. Bell names this vision of power 'redemptive hegemony', that is, 'saving power'. It denotes

> the way in which reality is experienced as a natural weave of constraint and possibility, the fabric of day-to-day dispositions and decisions experienced as a field for social action. Rather than embracing an ideological vision of the whole, it conveys a biased, nuanced rendering of the ordering of power so as to facilitate the visioning of personal empowerment through activity in the perceived system.[15]

Thus worship is crafted in such a way that it forms in the participating bodies a disposition towards a particular ordering of saving power. By engaging in the practice of worship, the participating bodies rehearse this ordering of saving power, in turn shedding light upon their experience of the rest of reality. Worship does not do this by presenting an ideological vision, but by 'rendering the ordering of power' so that participants may experience personal empowerment and their place in what I have called a 'geography of sacred power'.

These four characteristics of ritual practice, when applied to worship, sharpen our need to understand it as much more than a backdrop for the enactment of myths or the conveyance of ideas. In sum, worship forms the whole person, attitudinally and not only intellectually, by rehearsing our selves, our souls, our bodies through verbal and nonverbal means, engaging us in a semblance of the Reign of God. This takes place without worship telling us what it is doing, nor how, but rather presenting these behaviors as 'the way things ought to be'.

The tools of worship

Let us go one level deeper: What elements are at the disposal of worship in order to present this semblance of the Reign, teaching us new habits of thought and feeling? What are the ritual 'tools' at its disposal? By ritual tools I mean the aspects or elements out of which worship is *crafted*.[16] For worship is not a natural thing, growing on trees, but a specific type of human *artifact*.

'What do we need in order to make eucharist?' is a question often found on the lips of Christian educators. The most essential element in worship, after God, is not the priest but the Christian People. I say this at the outset because one of the great temptations of clergy is to take the People of God for granted. But without the people, there is no priest, nor steeple!

The next most essential elements of worship *are not* the font, ambo, and altar, nor the water, Bible, or bread and wine, but the *symbolic actions* of the People of God responding ritually to God's summons to gather with the divine presence. In the celebration of the Holy Eucharist, for example, these can be listed as:

1 Gathering in response to God's call.
2 Listening to God.

3 Responding to what God has to say.
4 Asking God to do something in light of what has been said.
5 Thanking God and asking for the Spirit.
6 Eating together.
7 Being sent out by God to serve the world and heal it.

These seven actions of the eucharistic liturgy are our ritual means for forming Christians in and through the liturgy. Of course, these actions *may* involve specific items of furniture – font, ambo, altar – and specific objects such as water, books, and food. However, these do not have meaning in themselves, but *as they are employed in the context of the assembly's symbolic actions rehearsing the Reign of God.*

But wait: Is not worship foundationally *God's* action? Absolutely. It is God who calls us together, proclaims something, listens to our prayers, initiates and supports conversion, feeds us, and sends us into the world to heal it. God even can and sometimes does create worship – and even anti-worship – to shake us up and make the divine presence unavoidably clear. God, however, does this *through* our very human actions of gathering, listening, answering, thanking, eating, and sending in order to do what God wills to do with us: rehearse us in the habits of the Reign, so we can receive it when it comes. Thus, what we can and must ask is how the *assembly responds* to God's initiative through its liturgical action.[17]

I wish to stress that the People of God in Christ, the Church, is the main *actor* in worship, carrying out these symbolic actions. Thus we are the main instruments of liturgical formation in and through worship. Our texts, music, décor, ceremonial, sacred objects, etc., all *assist* us as an assembly in our work of embodying and rehearsing life in the Reign of God.

All the meaningfulness of everything that transpires in worship derives from the mystery that is the assembly, the Church. Our place of meeting, our sacred books and their pulpit or ambo, our table and its meal, our font, are holy, due to this primacy of the assembly in worship, responding to God's initiative. Thus we

9

can say that the *importance of every other aspect of worship is relative to the assembly's ritual actions.*

An illustration of this point, if I may. During the 1995 meeting of the International Anglican Liturgical Consultation in Dublin, Ireland, Bishop David Gitari of Kenya reminded us that all our talk of chancels during our discussion about the ordination rites did not make much sense to him, for, as he said, 'Half of my congregations meet under trees!' And, we would surely add, their worship is no less formative, no less the presence of God among humans, no less a sign of the Reign, no less the New Jerusalem. There, under those trees, the assembly is forming itself into a holy temple of living stones and forming new members of the Body of Christ. It is the assembly, and what it *does* in worship is formative. In the hands of the Christian assembly, the ordinary actions of gathering, listening, sharing, interceding, giving thanks, eating and drinking, and walking out are turned into Spirit-filled actions, as they are carried out as if we were living in full awareness of the presence of God.

The assembly's work of worship

The assembly, then, is the main actor in worship. Allow me now to point out three interesting aspects of the assembly's work of worship.

First, in many ways great and small, the actions of worship, though ordinary, are also constructed; for liturgy does not grow on trees. You do not find it in nature. You must *craft* it.

Additionally, like most artwork and like all ritual, the work of worship is evocative rather than logical. We are not gathering in order to have a coherent, intellectually logical experience of tenets. Our actions have a dream-like logic rather than a didactic clarity. This is an important point, for in liturgy we are formed in meta-logical ways, through suggestion, resonance, analogy, and metaphor more than through clearly defined, unequivocal actions and words allowing for only one interpretation. Thus eating and drinking together in memory of Jesus is a sign of

God's radical inclusion of outcasts in the Reign. But it is also a sign of the New Jerusalem, of Heaven, of the Last Supper, of the Messianic Banquet, etc. Baptism is a bath, but it is also a death and rebirth, the Pasch of Jesus lived symbolically in our own bodies, a possession by the Spirit, our own epiphany as sons and daughters of the Most High.

For this reason, actions – including spoken language – that can only mean one thing tend to impoverish worship. Worship proceeds analogically and metaphorically, at times even irrationally, the way dreams do, and we cannot succeed at grasping its meaning by insisting that it be logical. It is not meant to be logical; it is meant to be *evocative*.

Finally, our gathering for worship, though crafted out of ordinary elements, is *distinct* from other gatherings. Our speech is more or less patterned. Our leadership is officially designated, even if temporarily. Our place of worship is in some way marked as a special place even if just for an hour. Worship presents itself to us as something 'special', even 'sacred', different from everyday life.

Thus the next question: What tools does the assembly have to craft its work of liturgy? What are the symbolic means at the disposal of the assembly? Where do we acquire our actions, gestures, movement, decoration, music, words, translations, prayers, etc.? The Almy catalogue?

The first and easiest answer is, of course, from our past. We inherit the tools of worship by worshipping in an unbroken chain over the centuries. This connection to the past is vital, for worship must present itself to us as *'the way we have always done it'*, as something that predates us as participants, older and greater than us, and outlasting us. Only in this way can we give ourselves over to it in a willing suspension of disbelief.

But the past also presents a challenge. As the assembly develops its repertoire of liturgical actions and props over time, it tends to depend upon the originally expressive forms – which were at one time easily grasped by those present – and holds on to them even though their expressiveness and transparency have now become dull and opaque. Thus the faithful Anglo-Catholic thinks that the whole world knows what a Gradual Psalm is when in fact most people are mystified by the term, for, as a wide-eyed parishioner once told me, 'We do not say it slowly!' The same faithful Anglo-Catholic will advocate the need for 'liturgical formation' as the process of explaining our liturgical lingo so people may then join us in worship meaningfully. As we shall soon see, however, this is not true liturgical formation any more than it is true evangelism. At best it is liturgical *in*formation or explication.

Indeed, if there is a task urgently before us as a church, it is to avail ourselves of the tools of worship present in our own local cultures and our own time and places. As a church we must fashion our worship with tools that are patently meaningful not only to those of us steeped in the recondite terminology of liturgy but, perhaps more crucially, to the culture in which each of us lives, moves, and has our being. Otherwise we will run the risk of becoming liturgical curators rather than craftspeople making worship from generation to generation. This brings us to the relationship between culture, worship, and liturgical formation.

Liturgical formation, inculturation and deformation

In this light, the work of the International Anglican Liturgical Consultation in the area of the inculturation of worship has tremendous importance. Although our York statement from 1989 was perhaps originally drafted regarding worship in cultures other than Anglo-Saxon, we in the United States are increasingly aware that our worship is not inculturated even in the contemporary white, English-speaking dominant culture of the United States.

In that York Statement we wrote:

True inculturation implies a willingness in worship to listen to culture, to incorporate what is good and to challenge what is alien to the truth of God. It has to make contact with the deep feelings of people. It can only be achieved through an openness to innovation and experimentation, an encouragement of local creativity, and a readiness to reflect critically at each stage of the process . . . The liturgy, rightly constructed, forms the People of God, enabling and equipping them for their mission of evangelism and social justice in their culture and society.

. . . Provinces should be ready both to treasure their received ways and also to reflect critically on them in the light of their own cultures. They should be wary lest sheer conservatism in liturgy, or an over-dependence upon uses from elsewhere, in fact become a vehicle of cultural alienation, making Anglican worship a specialist cult, rather than a people's liturgy.[18]

I cannot overemphasize how dangerous is the failure to incarnate our worship in the local time, place, and culture. Often with the passing of centuries our oblivion – if not disdain – of our local cultures can turn formative worship into a deforming event, shaping a people who think they can be close to God while remaining far from the everyday world, or who expect the arrival of the Reign to be *only* an interior event, between the individual's heart and God.

But there is an additional danger. Since worship takes place in the subjunctive mode (we worship 'as if' we were in the Reign of God), the exotic otherness of a liturgy from another time, place, and culture can be too easily be confused with the radical otherness of God's Reign. Worshipping 'as if we were in Restoration England' is not necessarily worshipping 'as if we were in the presence of God'. 'That was a wonderful service Father: I felt like I was in heaven!' is wonderful praise, but unfortunately the person is describing an experience of dying and going to King's College, Cambridge. Some Roman Catholics face a similar challenge, confusing the Reign of God with the Latin *Te Deum* in the *finale* of the first act of Verdi's *Tosca*.

The challenge is particularly acute in former colonies, where British worship is often indistinguishable from the Reign of God. An assembly doing this in the formerly colonial setting is being formed by a liturgical experience in which they must move, dress, act, sound, and sing like English men and women in order to rehearse the Reign of God and proclaim that they are sons and daughters of the Most High. It's a kind of ecclesiastical Mikado.

The depth of liturgical deformation in these situations is only recently dawning upon the church. For these un-inculturated liturgies *are the ritualization of colonialism*, patterning the bodies of the participants into submission to a foreign power. More dangerously, since these participants are being transported to another culture, at another time, in another place, it is very easy for them to confuse this (to them) exotic otherness of British worship with the Reign of God. This is a form of idolatry – worshipping another culture, or another time or place, instead of the living God present in their own culture, time, and place. This idolatrous liturgy, being sacramental, is also efficacious: it forms (I should say deforms) the participants. It conditions human bodies to be a different people – not in the Gospel sense, not as citizens in the New World, but as allies of the invading cultural powers, internalizing colonial views of themselves in their unconscious attitudes. I do not need to point out the disastrous effects of this for the spread of the liberating Gospel of Jesus Christ.

Therefore it is not enough to say that the assembly's tools for crafting its worship come only from history. They must also come from the present time, the concrete place, the local culture. Only then, when the assembly crafts its worship rooted in tradition yet fully employing contemporary symbolic actions, objects, texts, and music, can the participants be formed into what they celebrate: the living Body of Christ. Otherwise, all their energy must be dedicated to deciphering the meaning of foreign actions, words, songs, etc., so that once they have learned to decode them, *then* and only then, they can experience worship.

It is sad that this kind of explication of liturgical ciphers from another time, place, and culture so often passes for liturgical formation. Sad and dangerous, for some people even think that it is appropriate for the liturgy to trade in these arcane forms, in the service of 'mystery'. Louis Weil, however, used to remind us in class that worship is about a mystery *revealed*; it is not supposed to be mystification of the assembly.

In light of the foregoing, it is clear that we must learn to take a hard look at the liturgical practices to which we submit our congregations and ask such questions as, 'Is this how *our* people in this time, place, and culture gather? listen? share meaning? pray?' 'Is this how our people give thanks, share a meal, get sent out to serve?' Only when we can answer these questions with a secure 'yes' can our worship form rather than deform.

Additionally, we must be courageous enough to ask of every liturgical detail we have received from history, Is this universal, or was it a local expression? What did it mean to the people back then? What does it mean to us today? Has the meaning changed? What would be today's dynamic equivalent of the original practice? Does the service actually express what we say it means to us? Is this meaning-to-us congruent with its meaning-to-the-tradition? This process of deconstructing our liturgical inheritance while constructing it anew in our own culture, time, and place is perhaps the main challenge to liturgical formation today. I'm sorry to say, it is largely absent from the liturgical training offered to church leaders in our seminaries.

To sum up, we can say that worship forms worshippers by their act of worshipping. In it, whole persons – body, mind, and spirit – rehearse a repertoire of actions, postures, movements, feelings, attitudes, and ideas engaged as characteristic of the Reign of God. This rehearsal of the Reign, being symbolic and sacramental, is also efficacious and can thus form – and deform – the participants. In order to avoid a deformed church, the ritual tools of worship must come from the local time, place, and culture, *and* from history, provided these latter are ever examined closely and renewed in relation to our present so that they may be immediately apprehended by the participants, especially the new ones, *without explication*. To refuse to do this while wringing our hands about our lack of growth in membership is at best short-sighted, at worst a form of denial.

Personal reflection and meaning-making

'But what about mystagogy?'[19] you will say. And I welcome the question, for worship forms us not only in the act of worship (*theologia prima*, or first-order theology) but also through the myriad ways in which we reflect upon the worship experience and relate it to our personal and corporate everyday lives (*theologia secunda*, or second-order theology), and it is to this second aspect of liturgical formation that I now turn.[20]

In the early church, reflection upon the meaning of worship took the form of an explanation by the bishop of the meaning of the liturgical actions after they were experienced by the newly baptized for the first time. As the church continued to develop, however, this reflection has also developed in myriad ways, from the writings of Pseudo-Dionysius to Teresa of Avila, to Cursillo weekends, to Monika Hellwig's *The Eucharist and the Hunger of the World*.[21] The wealth of Christian reflection upon what we do in worship is enormous. Most of this reflection is written. At least in the First World, it is available to seminarians. What strikes me, however, is how conspicuously lacking in most congregations is the opportunity for worshippers *to share reflections about their own experience of worship and its meaningfulness to them.*

The mother of a recently baptized infant said to me last year, 'I wasn't too excited about meeting with the sponsors and the catechists *after* the baptism, but my husband and I were thrilled that a small party had been organized, and we were invited to watch a video of our son's baptism and to share what the experience had meant to us.'

Authors of books on worship often forget that *the liturgical experience is supposed to mean something to the participants.* Thomas Aquinas understood this well, writing that the sacraments of the new law effect what they mean, adding, 'They effect it by meaning it.'[22] It follows, then, that without the ability to mean something to the participants, the sacraments are *not efficacious*, not because God, in a fit of pique, closes down shop and walks away, but because the participants, unable to suspend disbelief before something meaningless, in order to enter into the semblance created by the rite, cannot appropriate the divine gift of grace offered to them through the liturgical action.

Too often we fall into the trap of thinking that the meaning of worship is contained in a book sitting in the library. The meaning of the Eucharist for Augustine may well be in the library, but the meaning of the Eucharist for Juan Oliver is living right here, in this body. For, as Michael Aune has written, 'meaning is always meaning to someone'.

> Within the humanities and social sciences . . . notions of the neutral observer, a neutral language, and a world of brute facts are giving way to alternative interests and approaches. The task now is how to understand better human expression as it occurs in particular contexts and what and how it means for those whose expression it is. What this broad shift involves for those of us working in liturgical studies is to recognize, finally, that the meanings of Christian worship are always 'meanings-to-someone'.[23]

Thus, before it can be systematized into an absolute statement like '*this* is the meaning of the Eucharist', meaning must be developed, discovered, or accepted by a concrete person, in his or her specific historical co-ordinates of time, place, culture, economics, politics, and intellectual assumptions, etc. Even then, meaning is not a self-existing being floating around in the atmosphere. Rather, like chairs and tables – like worship itself – it is a human artifact, constructed by human beings.

Making meaning consists of finding a connection between one thing and another, and this is something only each of us can create. It cannot be done for us by Augustine, unless we freely decide to trust him and simply accept his meaning. But even then, we are in charge. Liturgical meaning is a connection that we find between the liturgical action and our lives. I have borrowed Suzanne Langer's term *import* to point to the meaningfulness of a symbolic action and the claims that it lays upon us and upon our daily lives.

If the Eucharist means to me, for example, that all are welcome to Christ's table, it will put a claim on me every time I try to reject someone in my life. Over time, I can develop and grow this meaning of the Eucharist *for me*. Into that process, Augustine and the great cloud of witnesses that as a Christian I belong to, may – and should – chime in, feed, critique, and enlighten my work of meaning-making; but when push comes to shove, if I do not make meaning, no one can give it to me. This process of making meaning from our experience of worship is at the core of liturgical formation and is second in importance only to crafting a liturgy in which the Reign of God may be experienced and rehearsed without explication. Furthermore, the process is both individual and communal: I make meaning from *my* liturgical experience and *we* also make meaning from *our* liturgical experience.

Perhaps it is clearer now why liturgical inculturation is so crucial to liturgical formation. For the liturgical experience to be available as an experience from which participants can create meaning with an import on their everyday lives, it must be built from elements of the local time, place, and culture. Another example: my friend Pedro cannot make meaning from his liturgical experience. He cannot because the worship to which he is exposed has no relation to his culture or tastes, which are characterized by fast, guitar-driven rhythms; a profusion of colorful statues of the saints, flowers, and candles; processions; and prayers written in baroque Spanish. He finds Anglo worship deadly boring; the music tedious; the immobility and reserve of the people weird; the sermons abstract and cold, lacking in emotion; the polyester vestments badly put together (he's a tailor). He associates organ music with funeral parlors. For Pedro worship is meaningless. *No le importa:* it has no import for him. Thus, he cannot engage in *theologia prima*, let alone *secunda*.

'How about an instructed liturgy?' a friend said when I told him about this. But an instructed liturgy is only explication of the arcane, a clear sign that the symbolic actions of worship are no longer communicating to the participants, and thus they cannot present the Reign of God to the participants unless they have had long, long formation in this – to them foreign – worship. Clearly we cannot expect our assemblies to develop vibrant reflection upon liturgy if their liturgies are not inculturated.

But even assuming that the liturgy is of the local place, time, and culture, what can or should we do in order to support pastorally this process of personal meaning-making? I have several suggestions.

First, assemblies might be encouraged to take rites of passage (pastoral rites) more seriously. It is a shame that we baptize, confirm, heal, reconcile, and marry people with so little preparation and emotional investment, with nary a thought of reflection upon their experience of the rite. It's a pity, for these persons are – we hope – going through life passages that are profoundly meaningful to them. So my first suggestion is: *Plan both preparation for rites and reflection on them afterwards.*

Second, *do not expect the meaning to be crafted prior to the rite.* The meaning even of the honeymoon cannot be known until *after* the honeymoon. Preparation for a rite is one thing; articulating its meaning by the participants another, better done afterwards.

Third, *leave Augustine in the library for now.* Meaning-making is the work of the participant, not the work of the priest, nor the novice master, nor the seminary professor. The participant, the student, the seminarian, the lay person preparing for a sacrament, *they* are the makers of meaning. Of course, you should bring Augustine into the conversation eventually. But when? Not when you want to show off your wide learning; not when the person clams up and won't share; not when you have to prove him or her mistaken. Only when Augustine echoes or expands what the person is saying. Then the participant discovers that other Christians across time and space and culture have made similar meanings out of *their* experience. If you wait till this moment to bring in Augustine, you will have opened up a door for the participant, leading him or her into the riches of tradition, a tradition that he or she will go on to dialogue with for the rest of his or her life in trust rather than fear.

Fourth, *meaning-making takes community.* It is very difficult to articulate a meaning and its import if there is no one to talk to. Yet in our individualistic first world, many, clergy and laity alike, assume that this is most easily done in private. It is not. I know that clergy take our responsibility for pastoral care seriously, but frankly, there is no substitute for a group of peers talking to each other about the meaning of what they have experienced. By sharing the meaningfulness of the rite and its import with each other, participants in such a group enrich and cross-fertilize both their meaning and its import. These groups are best led by trained lay members of the congregation.

Fifth, *ritualize the process of preparation for and reflection upon rites.* During preparation for baptism, pray by name for the candidates and the parents and sponsors during the intercessions; the same with confirmands, couples engaged to be married, etc. Bring them before the congregation and pray over them. Make them visible. In these ways the congregation learns that preparation for rites is the norm rather than the exception, and that reflection upon worship is the right and duty of all Christians.

Sixth, *preach on the meaning of worship.* Do not explicate what mystifies. Change or get rid of it! Instead, delve into the real mystery hidden from all time and now revealed: the reconciliation of all things in Christ and that great mystery, the relationship between Christ and his Church. These, and the sacraments as mysteries, are revealed, but not obvious. It is not obvious (and can never be) how we, the bread and wine, and the risen Christ are all one. It is not obvious that Jesus handed over his Spirit and then water and blood flowed out, and what this has to do with us as an assembly. It is not obvious why the Holy Spirit was breathed upon the disciples on the first Easter afternoon. It is not obvious that the eucharistic meal has something to do with the hunger of millions on our planet. This is a depth of meaning that must be unravelled, unpacked, and shared by the growing Christian with the help of other Christians and their pastors, group facilitators, preachers, etc.

Finally, but most importantly, *connect the work of liturgy to the work of justice.* I do not mean preach about it. That's good, but not enough. A story comes to mind.

Years ago I was the vicar of a tiny mission in a hippie town in California. Fifteen of us gathered weekly in a tiny cottage church by the shore. One Sunday, Sunshine Appleby (yes, that is her name) grabbed me over coffee and asked, in her impertinent 'I won't let you get away, Father,' tone, 'Juan, how come we are not feeding the homeless in town?' Sunshine is one tough lady. She'd been catechized and baptized as an adult by Phillip Berrigan in the sixties. 'Nothing to stop *you* from doing it!' I shot back, tired and, frankly, not looking forward to yet another project.

Two weeks later Sunshine announced that the restaurants in the area had agreed to give her their uncooked food on Saturday nights, and she would be leaving it by the church door in bags at dawn on Sundays. The homeless would come and get what they needed. Thus began a ministry that is still going on. Eventually the homeless folks asked if they could cook in the church kitchen on Thursday night and eat in the only space available – the nave. We agreed, and once a week, the chapel became a dining room, the chairs reorganized along a large ping-pong table.

Holy Week was approaching, and we discussed what to do for Maundy Thursday. I talked about celebrating the Eucharist in the context of a full meal. Sunshine brought up foot washing. Everyone was on board until it became evident that Sunshine was assuming that the Maundy Thursday liturgy would take place in the midst of the dinner of the homeless folks. For once I recognized someone else's genius.

Maundy Thursday came and we gathered around a large potluck, explained what we were about to do, and sang, shared scripture, washed feet, and shared a eucharistic potluck with our guests, who took it all in good humour, wide-eyed and amused. Years after I left the mission I learned that the Thursday dinner had been moved to noon on Sundays, immediately following the regular celebration of the Eucharist.

I do not bring this up to suggest that you should do the same. That happened in that place at that time in that culture. But I do want to stress that the liturgy is not supposed to merely point to justice or talk about justice; the liturgy is to *enact* justice, for it is an embodied rehearsal of the Reign of God, not a message about it. If I may paraphrase James Empereur, we do not want a liturgy about justice; we want a liturgy that *does* justice.[24] The connection between worship and justice must be tangible in the worship event itself and not only as its intellectual content.

Intellectual ideas and liturgical formation

So far I have emphasized liturgical craft, inculturation, and personal reflection upon rites. Some of you may be thinking that I am somehow anti-intellectual. Allow me to disabuse you. I cannot leave unmentioned the role of ideas and concepts in liturgical formation. I have said very little so far about this because I wanted to drive home the importance of the liturgy as a crafted artifact; of its incarnation in a given time, place, and culture; and of reflection upon our experience of the liturgical action and its import in our lives. I would now like to turn to the role of intellectual insight.

I mentioned earlier our historical treasure-house of reflection upon the meaning of our worship. This treasure-house is enormously valuable. Let me remind us, however, that these treasures come from different times, different places, and often different cultures. Thus, just because I *like* a phrase of Chrysostom's does not mean that I understand it as he did, much less that it is necessarily true in my own place, time, and culture. We must therefore learn to *interpret* our treasures from tradition as much as our worship and, of course, Scripture, so we can build ideas and insights appropriate to our time, place, and culture. This is not *less* intellectual work, but *more*. If we do this well, our ideas will be worthy of our forebears; if we do it shoddily, we will betray them.

I say this because at our last meeting, in San Francisco, some of you were rather astonished at my suggestion that theology is culturally constructed. Let me reassure you that the object of theology, God, is beyond culture, time, and space, and that God's grace and goodwill towards creation are constant and unchanging. But *we* are not, and cannot be, outside a given culture, place, and time. Human understandings of God and God's actions can by definition only approximate God, and being human, these understandings are always affected not only by our time, place, and culture, but by every aspect of our situation in life: political, philosophical, economic, sexual, etc.

This means that when we go to drink from the wells of tradition, we must be very careful to drink in such a way that we can assimilate what we take in, without the risk of it passing through us like a purgative. For active meaning-making from our liturgical experience is *not* the parroting of old ideas but the building of *our* ideas about the meaning of our worship experience in the light of tradition properly appropriated. To be able to contribute to this project, traditional intellectual concepts must *also* be deconstructed and inculturated, or they will not be assimilated by our contemporaries without the benefit of doctoral degrees. We cannot say that we understand Chrysostom's phrase if we do not understand its connections to his time, place, and culture as well as the politics, philosophy, theology, economics, and gender constructions of his time.

I say this out of a concern that Anglican liturgical theology is still largely a first-world, male craft. As such, it has its limitations, and its claims to universality must be re-examined, just as we must examine the colonizing practice of exporting English liturgy. Where is the Anglican liturgical theology of African parishes? of Asian rural poor congregants? Where is the reflection upon the meaning of worship for Latin-American Anglicans in their efforts to differentiate from Roman Catholics? We badly need them.

If we do not include these other Christian theologies in our liturgical theology as Anglicans we will be doing intellectually what we have so often done liturgically: making the world into our image and likeness, insisting that others live in our ecclesiastical ghetto, a foreign, old place and time, crafting worship and theology according to our ways and thoughts. This can be very beautiful! Its very exoticism will tempt us, again, to confuse that exotic place, be it Byzantine Constantinople or Restoration England, with the Reign of God.

The work of liturgical formation is at the core of the dynamics of church growth in Christian maturity as well as numbers. It is also at the core of the pastoral care of both seasoned participants and newcomers. In order to do this work, however, our worship must be locally crafted, inculturated by employing elements from the local time, place, and culture. It must be also be accompanied by proactive processes of personal and communal reflection upon our experience of it so as to develop a deep personal sense of its meaning and import upon our lives.

23

A final note about seminary education. Perhaps some of you thought at the outset that I would be speaking about the liturgical formation of seminarians. I have not so far because liturgy, as taught in seminaries, is often presented as something invariable, a freeze-dried dinner needing only a microwave oven. This is not liturgical formation in any sense of the term as I have used it today. For seminarians to be formed liturgically, they must have hands-on experience in crafting worship in a safe environment, with the luxury of being able to make mistakes. They must grapple with the inculturation of Anglican worship in their own time, place, and culture, and they must reflect personally upon their experience of worship, assisted by the process of delving deep into the treasure-house of liturgical history and theology, subjecting the intellectual treasures that feed us to a process of deconstruction and rebuilding in their local contexts. This, however, is not the exclusive province of seminaries. Seminarians share these needs with all the People of God. As future priests and deacons, however, they must also engage in practice and reflection upon the role of presider and deacon in relation to the liturgical formation of the assembly. It is a tall order, I know, but hopefully it will enable the genesis of the church among all languages, peoples, and nations – including people in London and New York.

Notes

1 If memory serves me, the term was coined by the Revd Canon Robert Brooks, who by then had been engaged for some time in the rediscovery of the catechumenate by the Episcopal Church.

2 Tertullian, *Apologeticus*, XVIII, 4.

3 Eph. 4.13b.

4 See especially Louis-Marie Chauvet, 'The Liturgy in Its Symbolic Space', *Liturgy and the Body*, eds Louis Chauvet and François Kabasele Lumbala (New York: Orbis Books, 1995), pp. 29–39.

5 Catherine Bell, *Ritual Theory, Ritual Practice* (New York: Oxford University Press, 1992), p. 83. See also her *Ritual: Perspectives and Dimensions* (New York: Oxford University Press, 1997).

6 See my 'The Look of Common Prayer: The Anglican Liturgical Place in Anglo-American Culture' (PhD dissertation, Berkeley, CA: The

Graduate Theological Union, 2006). I have taken the term *semblance* from the work of the philosopher of art Suzanne Langer.

7 So, for example, John the Solitary, *Letter to Hesychius* 19, 26; Babai, *Letter to Syriacus*, 56; Isaac of Nineveh, *Discourse XXII*; and Joseph the Visionary, *On the Stirrings of the Mind During Prayer*, all in Sebastian Brock, *The Syriac Fathers on Prayer and the Spiritual Life* (Kalamazoo, MI: Cistercian Publications, 1987).

8 Heb. 12.18–19, 22–24 (NKJV).

9 Pierre Bourdieu, *Outline of a Theory of Practice*, trans. Richard Nice (Cambridge: Cambridge University Press, 1977).

10 Bell, *Ritual Theory*, p. 79.

11 Bourdieu, *Outline of a Theory of Practice*, p. 124.

12 Bell, *Ritual Theory*, p. 82.

13 Ibid.

14 Ibid., p. 109.

15 Ibid., p. 84.

16 I am grateful to Daniel Stevick for this term: *The Crafting of Liturgy* (New York: Church Hymnal Corp., 1990).

17 I am indebted to Lizette Larson-Miller for her insight that the liturgy is at bottom, God's action, even though it may take place through the instrumentality of the assembly.

18 'The York Statement', cited in Paul Gibson, 'International Anglican Liturgical Consultations: A Review'. http://www.anglicancommunion. org/ministry/liturgy/docs/ialcreview.cfm; accessed 05/06/2009.

19 Mystagogy, or 'leading into the mysteries', is the classical term for the process of developing one's personal meaning of the experience of a given rite.

20 *Theologia prima* and *secunda* are terms developed by Aidan Kavanagh, taking a clue from Eastern Christianity, which considers worship the theological act par excellence (*theologia prima*), upon which we then build a more or less systematic theological reflection (*theologia secunda*).

21 New York: Paulist, 1976; 2nd edn, revised and expanded, Kansas City, MO: Sheed and Ward, 1992.

22 '*Sacramenta significando efficiunt*', in Thomas Aquinas, *Super libros sententiarum Magistri Petri Lombardi*, Book IV, distinctio 23, quaestio 1, art. 2, qc 2s, c2.

23 Michael B. Aune, 'Worship in an Age of Subjectivism Revisited', *Worship* 65 (1991): 225. For the expression 'meanings-to-someone', see Ronald Grimes, *Ritual Criticism* (Columbia, SC: University of South Carolina Press, 1990), p. 42.

24 James L. Empereur and Christopher G. Kiesling, *The Liturgy That Does Justice* (Collegeville, MN: Liturgical Press, 1990).

2

LITURGICAL EDUCATION AND FORMATION FROM AN AFRICAN PERSPECTIVE

Solomon Amusan

Preamble

I have some confessions to make at the beginning of this chapter.

1 While preparing this chapter, there was confusion as to what could be regarded as liturgical education and formation from an African perspective, since the universally accepted origin of the Christian liturgy is the western world. Could it not be a self deceit to present anything from an African perspective? After a protracted struggle, I decided to put this before you. If it falls below your expectation, I have no apology. However, I wish you to consider it as part of the learning process of a student of liturgy like me.

2 It must be noted here that any comprehensive discussion of this topic would require prolonged collaboration with specialists in the history and development of liturgy in African Traditional Religion. However, the urgency of the question does not give room for the very exhaustive and meaningful

discussion I should have loved to have. Therefore I want to say that the commentary I present to you is a purely private venture and has no serious authority. If it appears to be a rather personal commentary, it is the only sort I could present for now. I hope another opportunity will become available for better presentation. This is not a self-condemnation but a confession in order not to feel disappointed.

3 I must also add that the intention of this presentation is not to superimpose any of these ideas on you as the only way. Rather, it is just to arouse your interest and re-awaken your spirit in this regard.

4 The interest of liturgical education compels me to embark upon an investigation of the concept and practice of what I describe as liturgical formation and education in African religion, pointing out the likely liturgical elements we can derive to ascertain their contribution positively or negatively to the concept of Christian liturgy.

5 For easy reference, the Yoruba tribe in Nigeria will be the focus of this presentation. I am from this tribe, and the tribe has a larger percentage of Anglican members than any other tribe in Nigeria. Among Yoruba people awareness of pre-Christian religion is one of the factors encouraging a lively practice of Christianity in Yorubaland.[1] It is true that traditional religion is dying,[2] but as we shall see some of its practices have found their way into Christian liturgical practice in Yorubaland.

Yoruba religious practice

As we cannot discuss the liturgical formation of any religious group without looking at the traditional religious practice of that community, it is therefore appropriate to go to the root of the religious practice of the Yoruba people. It is necessary to make it abundantly clear from the outset that Africa in general and Nigeria in particular received Christianity and Christian liturgy from the colonial masters. Hence there could be no Christian liturgical formation as a point of reference; rather we have to look at the African religious practice.

The Nigerians and particularly the Yoruba to whom Westerners brought Christianity in the nineteenth century were already a religious people.[3] The idea of worshipping God was not new to them. They had various intermediary deities through whom they offered their worship to the supreme deity. Among these gods are Sango,[4] Oya,[5] Egungun,[6] and Ogun,[7] to mention just a few. The missionaries, when they arrived, chose to describe the Yoruba people as idolatrous, as, for example, Anna Hinderer:

> Yoruba whose religion hitherto is a system of idolatry, in which a multitude of idols, above all, Ifa, the god of divinations, who is presented and consulted by means of palm-nuts, are worshipped as mediators between the people and the supreme God who they acknowledge.[8]

Hinderer's observation includes an admission that Nigerians are religious people.

John Mbiti rightly insists that Africans are not religiously illiterate.[9] According to Adiele Eberechukwu Afigbo, by and large the Yoruba people have established religion 'which was centred around the worship of Supreme God known as Olódumarè' through deities which they regarded as intermediaries between them and the Supreme God.[10]

The subject of Yoruba religion is immense, and there is a large literature devoted to various aspects of its thought-world.[11] Rather than attempt to sum up the investigations, we shall concentrate here on Yoruba ritual practice, not only because this is a more manageable undertaking, but also because it is directly relevant to our topic and even more because it is in its rites that we see a religious system most clearly at work.

Worship among Yoruba people

At the heart of Yoruba culture is the making of sacrifice or offering of gifts even of the smallest kind.[12] Such transactions permeate all social life and experience of the world. As Anna Hinderer has rightly observed, worship in general is intimately related to cultural experience as the way to express understanding of the Supreme Being or deity.

It is necessary for our present purpose to discuss the worship of a particular cult among Yoruba rather than discussing worship as a general theme. Ogun worshippers were selected for this purpose and carefully observed. We selected Ogun worship because its worship involves blood. The connotations of blood are, of course, very important to the theology of Eucharist. Ogun is a deity of potent attributes. He is regarded as the patron of all those professions which involve the use of iron, like driving (both private and commercial), blacksmithing, farming, and hunting. All the people involved are deemed to be connected with activities over which Ogun exercises patronage.[13]

The worship of the Ogun worshippers must be classed as liturgical, although they have no written texts because the traditional religion 'lacks written literature and depends mainly upon oral traditions'.[14] The lack of written literature is no barrier to the understanding of their approach to worship, since the order of worship has been preserved and transferred through the family priests from generation to generation. However, there is no unbiased documentary evidence of the liturgical worship of the Yoruba available for our study.

For this, there seem to be two reasons. Firstly, the Yoruba types of religion, as with other Nigerian religious behavior, were suppressed by the influence of the missionaries and the colonial authorities.[15] Secondly, the structure of liturgy is based on ancestral spirits related to each individual extended family and is not available for easy translation into contemporary circumstances. In spite of these limitations the available sources will provide helpful insights for the purpose of this paper.

The liturgical setting of Yoruba worship

The concept of liturgy is manifested in the way Yoruba worship. To them worship begins, controls, and ends all the affairs of life.[16] In everything they put deity at the centre. This concept is always put into action in the form of worship. Their worship is both private and public.[17] Their private worship includes, for example, individual morning worship at the shrine of the deity. No one will leave home without saying good morning to the deity. It takes the form of thanksgiving for protection during the night and asking for mercy during the day.

The public worship is more elaborate. It is a corporate act of the community of worshippers, and the priest dresses up suitably for this occasion.[18] The public worship usually takes place during festivals (further discussion will be presented on this topic later) and consists of song, dance, prayer, and offerings.

What is the structure of the 'liturgy' of the traditional worship of Ogun in Yorubaland? The opening act involves the worshipping community bringing kola-nuts to offer. Kola-nuts are offered to nearly all the gods[19] in Yorubaland, though there are a few who are held to prefer bitter kola-nuts. The nuts are broken and eaten by the worshippers as a sign of fellowship. 'So being shared with god, they form a bond of communion.'[20]

The traditional conduct of worship is treated with such caution and extreme care that custom is rigorously preserved. The worshippers are conscious that any omission in the normal order of service or any wrong word uttered or song not properly rendered during service could incur the displeasure of the deity and jeopardize the efficacy of worship.[21]

The constancy and frequency of this *oral order of service* have made it become a rigid order of worship followed by priests. For example, during an offering to Ogun the worshippers gather at the priest's house.[22] The 'Abogun' (the Ogun priest), and he alone, wears a garment decorated with cowries as a formal style of dress during the festival. We can describe this as liturgical vestment. Everyone begins to move, singing a processional hymn, to the Ogun shrine. They all dance amidst singing and drumming. The children lead the procession with the priest bringing up the rear with his lieutenants.

At the shrine, where are already some few worshippers, the same procedure of singing, drumming, and dancing in praise of

Ogun for the past provisions, joy, and protection vouchsafed by him is also followed. This functions as an act of invocation of the spirit of Ogun at the beginning of the worship. The main idea is that when they sing to praise Ogun, he will be moved to pay attention to the worshippers and thus heed their requests and wishes. Hence 'this aspect comes first in the order of their public worship'.[23]

After they are settled at the shrine, the priest steps forward before the shrine to start the ritual: first by citing some traditional narratives of Ogun (in form of songs of his praise) and then piercing the kola-nuts which are brought by the individual worshippers and in which everyone will partake as a sign of 'communion'. Another point to note is that a portion of the kola-nuts is taken home for those who could not attend the ceremony. (This is similar to the Christian practice of remembering the absent members at the communion.) They are later shared if the offering is accepted by Ogun. The sign of this acceptance is that the two halves of the split nut, cast up and forward, fall with one half facing up, the other down. If acceptance does not take place, a further oblation, as indicated by an oracle, must be made to placate Ogun.

Following this, intercession is made on behalf of the town, the 'Oba' or 'Bale' (the traditional ruler of the town or community), the state, and the country. The intercession is coupled with individual prayers with vows which precede the open testimony to answered prayers and fulfilment of vows. The interesting thing to note in the intercessory prayers is their resemblance to the intercessory prayers in the Orthodox liturgy. In the liturgy of St John Chrysostom, for example, there are various litanies. Apart from short litanies, there occur five major ones:

1 'Great' litany at beginning of service.
2 'Augmented' after Gospel.
3 'Of catechumens' after Augmented litany.
4 After the Great Entrance and before the Peace.
5 After the consecration and before the Lord's Prayer.[24]

As Awolalu rightly observes of this part of the rite, 'Prayer is a very important element in worship',[25] and this involves every worshipper praying to the god. After the prayers, either individual petition, intercessions, or biddings, a dog is beheaded and its blood is sprinkled on the shrine with palm oil and palm wine; this is followed by another round of prayers with vows, ending with blessing by the priest and a votive hymn.[26] At the end of the worship, they continue singing, drumming, and dancing for a period of time expressing their gratitude to Ogun.

As believers in the efficacy of prayers uttered by an individual person either in private or corporate worship, they offer prayers which comprise adoration, praise, thanksgiving, and petitions spontaneously rendered. This spontaneity of prayer in traditional liturgy makes it very different from the set prayers of the Christian liturgy, but the structure and segments of events are stable.

From the above account, it can be argued that it would be erroneous to say that the adherents of traditional religion have no order of worship or that their service is not liturgical. There are important elements and obvious features of their liturgy which are seldom practised in the Christian liturgy of the Eucharist. These include singing of native hymns, dancing, drumming, invocation, individual offertory, extempore prayers, and sharing of elements.

Theology of Yoruba liturgy

One point of note about the liturgy described above is the worshippers' total surrender of their life to the object of worship as expressed in their offering and prayers. This suggests that they believe that full responsibility for all human affairs belongs to the Supreme Being, and for their own part they are to act as ordered by their priests or diviners, who are regarded as interpreters of events and of the will of the Supreme Being.[27]

This belief is the principal factor that guides the life of the adherents of traditional religion, which was the holy religion before the advent of Christianity and Islam in Yorubaland. All circumstances of life are attributed to the Supreme Being, and the Supreme Being is believed to be transcendent,[28] even if that concept is naively expressed in terms of being in the sky. He is worshipped as being independent of the world which cannot exist without him. The Yoruba call him Olódumarè,[29] the Almighty and the Creator of the universe. Olódumarè is also understood to be related to the world and to control it, so they feel dependent on God and feel that they have a duty to worship him. This they express by means of praise and gifts offered in religious ceremonies.

One important aspect of Yoruba life is that the doctrine of their belief is married to their life. In day-to-day life they try to live in the way that they believe will please the Supreme Being. They uphold moral values and live by this standard. They believe they would anger the Supreme Being by living lower than the tenets of their faith, and when they feel they have angered him, they offer sacrifice to appease him.[30] They believe in prayer which they offer when making sacrifice before him, most prayers being of petition with vows: 'By praying, people express their dependence on God, and make their needs known to Him. Moreover, they think of God in personal terms.'[31] The Yoruba believe in 'communion' with God and other believers, seeing the universe as related to God and all in the universe related together. Thus you cannot separate yourself from the universe and from God.

They pray to Olódumarè through their deities anywhere and everywhere, believing unmistakably that the Supreme Being is living, his presence is felt anywhere, everywhere, and at all times in any situation and whatever the circumstances, either in joy or in distress.[32]

The Yoruba will say of God, 'A te rere kari aye; Ogbagba ti gba ara adugbo; Oba ti ngba eru ti ngba omo,' meaning, 'God who occupies the whole extent of the world, the Saviour who saves both slave and free-born.' This is the idea behind having no temple to localize the Supreme God in the Yoruba concept of the Supreme Being. God is universal and has absolute control of the universe. This is the cosmological view of the traditional religion.[33]

Another important area which needs mentioning about traditional liturgy is music. Anna Hinderer's journal frequently refers to the importance of music for the Yoruba people, although she fails to note the role of drumming as a means of communication and its importance in Yoruba life both socially and religiously.[34] We will now look briefly at the significance of music in worship.

The importance of native music in worship

The missionaries who came to Nigeria introduced Christianity and taught Christian doctrine, for which the Nigerian church continues to respect them. However, Christianity as they transmitted it was deeply tinged with western culture because it did not occur to many people to consider whether Christianity was compatible with or relevant to the Nigerian setting.[35] The missionaries conducted services in the only way they had themselves experienced, that is, in the English way. The worship of the Nigerian Anglican in particular was the English Anglican liturgy presented in European (English) fashion. Nigerian Christians worked hard to translate the English liturgy verbatim into Nigerian languages without considering the cultural relevance of the liturgy to the people.[36]

'It must be said here that if at the beginning anyone had had enough vision to suggest that while accepting Christianity, Nigerians did not need to throw away what was good and valuable in their own culture, such a person would have been accused of "rank heathenism" by the missionaries.'[37]

Thus today we find that in spite of the constitutional, liturgical, and dogmatic independence of the Anglican Church in Nigeria, the cool and sober ways of service as they were conducted are still the norm and standard by which the life of the church is ordered. People who form church opinion are inclined to feel that prestige attaches to association with the customs of churches abroad, and especially of the parent church in England.[38] And it is not easy for them to see themselves as attaining the goal of spiritual life unless they approach it by the way of some prefabricated English tradition.[39]

In all Nigerian culture, overt and warm expressions are natural, and excessive restraint and coldness in ritual action is incompatible with the corporate sensibility of the Nigerian peoples and emotionally alien to them. It is difficult therefore to identify the Nigerian mode of worship with the spiritual stability of the Anglican liturgy 'when hymns, psalms and canticles are translated from English into Nigerian languages and then sung to European tunes'.[40] Nigerian worshippers, Christians in particular, prefer something of a more domestic character, familiar and recognizable in their approach to their Creator in worship. They prefer singing native tunes to singing tunes borrowed from the English. They want to be spontaneous rather than to be rigid and static. They want to be emotional in celebrating God's presence in their midst with the beautiful music of their native tongues.

It is relevant to point out here that the early Christians in Nigeria did not welcome any foreign tune to sing praises to their God in worship. An indication of this can be gained from an article about Anna Hinderer:

> the Hinderers are left with their children who gathered around the harmonium to sing English and Yoruba hymns (English hymns translated into Yoruba language), unhappily mangled the Yoruba words beyond belief.[41]

The early converts had no choice but to accept the way of worship being imported into their culture. It would have been to the credit of the missionaries if they had allowed the worshippers to sing to their native style of music rather than European tunes.

No one who has had the opportunity of seeing a Nigerian festival, a sacrificial ceremony, or some other occasion such as marriage, a naming ceremony, or a funeral would disagree with the assertion that music is a dominant form of artistic expression in Nigerian social and religious life. Nor would they quarrel with the many descriptions that abound of the functional importance of its use as an outlet for emotion,[42] as a vehicle for verbal expression, and as a special means of communication and bonding.[43] Musicians are hired for funerals, naming and marriage ceremonies, and religious occasions during festivals when sacrifices are offered. One can hardly see any public worship without accompaniment of music involving drumming, dancing, and singing.[44]

It is one of the general practices of Nigerians that when people gather in any place for recreation or celebration or worship they turn the atmosphere to a joyous state that is itself sound-generating through various forms of rhythmic action, such as grinding stones or sticks, pounding, beating, or foot-tapping. It is worth noting that the resultant sound turns the situations into musical and emotional events. Therefore, in the day-to-day activities of Nigerians, it is very hard to separate music or singing from their lives.

In the orthodox churches in Nigeria and especially in the Anglican church, worshippers are denied native hymns with native drums and dancing because the present liturgy (1662 Book of Common Prayer) does not provide for this. The recently introduced 1996 Nigerian Book of Common Prayer tries to address this. If this book is not used, the 1662 liturgy makes the worship alien to Nigerians and their culture and also hampers the sense of worship itself. This makes many worshippers go to other denominations in their search for truly culturally fulfilling worship in the Christian church, as Wyatt Tee Walker notes:

> In many instances where individual churches have become imitative of the white man's worship (as in the Anglican church today) there has been a parallel loss of freedom of expression, enthusiasm, numerical strength, and sensitivity to the issues that affect the black masses.[45]

Religion and music have held, and still hold, an important place in the development of each other and in the spiritual growth of the Nigerian people. Music is described by Walker as central to the West African culture: 'As music is central to West African culture . . . music is one of the three major support systems in the black Church worship.'[46] Other attractive features include extemporaneous prayers which are related to their lives and appropriate sermons.

Music does not depend upon words for its appeal to human emotion. It speaks to hearts in a language that transcends racial and national barriers: 'Worshippers have appetite for music that is rhythmic and emotion-inducing',[47] which creates human feeling and emotion. In the Nigerian context, music goes hand in hand with religion, and religion expresses itself in music that appeals to the young and old, the rich and poor of all races. This is another important area of liturgical formation we can think of and try to develop.[48] If meaningful study of liturgical formation of any religious group has to be done, it must allow space for incorporation of the cultural heritage of the worshippers, for the 'deepest and most meaningful cultural heritage of persons must be identified, respected and built upon',[49] not in religious life alone but in every sphere of human endeavour.

Festival

At the advent of Christianity, the Yoruba Christians also observed the festivals related to their gods. Because of the interrelation between the religious and social life of the Yoruba, these festivals are observed by the Christians. Parratt and Doi describe this act as syncretism.[50]

There is no evidence to support the view that the observance of these festivals by Christians is based on any theological argument. Rather, such observance is due to social pressure to conform or at least to participate. In the case of the professed adherents of traditional religion, though significantly few in number, the situation may be different, and there probably are directly religious rather than merely sociological motivations. Among Christians the veneration of Ogun is attributed to economic motives, ensuring professional success, while veneration of the spirits of the ancestors is seen as socially beneficial since it connects the living with the heritage of the past and serves to strengthen the family unit. It can be further said that the elements of traditional religion still make a profound impression on some Christians.

Healing

Religious practice of the Yoruba is related to other spheres of life, among them healing. Healing in sickness is sought by offering

37

sacrifice to the relevant deity, after which the native medicine pre-
scribed by the priest along the traditional lines is applied. Native
medicine is believed to derive its origin from the deity who teaches
the priests how to prepare it.[51] It is said to achieve more than herb-
alism, effective though that itself often seems to be. Reasons for its
effectiveness may lie in genuine medicinal properties of the herbs
used according to the instruction given by the deity. Parratt and Doi
ascribe its effectiveness to suggestive effects upon the patients.[52]

In most cases a charm is prepared to be worn by the patients or
for protection from attack of disease or to prevent evil befalling the
user. Native medicine is not only for curing or preventing disease;
there are other types, such as medicine for good luck, for quick
sales of wares or to ensure prosperity, and for retentive memory,
and there are various other kinds. (This large subject must be regarded as beyond the scope of this paper, but it is indispensable for
the students of African Traditional Religion.) In Yoruba society,
where concern for health and the quest for healing and the use of
native medicine, curative or preventive, is so important a feature
of common experience, those aspects of Christian worship which
are concerned with healing must be acknowledged, affirmed, and
enhanced. James 5.14–16, as well as the healing ministry of Jesus,
establish the ministry of healing as an integral part of the Christian Church's sacramental worship. In addition to the specific rite
of anointing, every area of liturgy can exercise a healing role. This
is especially true of the Eucharist, which St Ignatius of Antioch
characterized as 'the medicine of immortality'.[53]

Conclusion

Like the churches in the West, the African churches have to decide
whether it is sufficient to incorporate local (in this case African)
traditions into the existing liturgy, or whether they should rather
seek, from the foundations, a genuinely Christian new inspiration
in African terms, thus creating a true African liturgical norm.

In 1983, the Church of Nigeria, Anglican Communion, in recognition of the crisis of liturgy in the province, extracted part of

The Alternative Service Book 1980 of the Church of England and adopted it as the *Liturgy of the Church of Nigeria*.[54] The justification for its introduction, as contained in its foreword, is that it uses contemporary language which is consistent with the Anglican tradition of worship in the language understood by the people. In the same foreword, the impression is given that the liturgy of the Church of Nigeria is not meant to replace the 1662 Order of the Administration of the Holy Communion – hereinafter referred to as the 1662 liturgy – which every ordained priest swears on oath to use. The 1983 liturgy of the Church of Nigeria is meant to be used as a supplement to the 1662 liturgy. It might be asked why there is a great reluctance to change the 1662 liturgy seeing that it does not originally belong to Nigeria but was imported to the country during the missionary period in the nineteenth century. This conservatism fosters the assumption that the 1662 liturgy has become sacrosanct and indispensable and that therefore it is the only fitting vehicle of liturgical expression. The situation remained until the 1996 Book of Common Prayer was introduced. The book was meant for experiment for five years to make room for revision after considering the comments of the users, both lay and ordained members of the church. Though the book borrowed from various sources and where possible Nigerian ideas were introduced, lack of thorough and deep liturgical education hindered our wish to throw away all things that could be regarded as foreign to Nigerian culture. I hope very soon things will work the way we wished.

This presentation is to underscore the vital role that pre-Christian religious practice plays in the liturgical formation we may have in Africa. We need to mention also that the Yoruba religious culture includes drumming, dancing, singing, and clapping; any attempt to introduce these elements into liturgical formation in Africa must respect the solemnity and dignity of the liturgy. This has often been summed up for Anglicans with the words 'decently and in order'. Such solemnity is significantly observed in certain traditional religious observances. Of course, singing and dancing can themselves be done solemnly and with great dignity. It would be possible fittingly to dance to the altar,

39

both at the offertory and also with the singing of choruses, during the reception of the elements.

Finally, I want to register my profound gratitude and deep
appreciation to the Steering Committee of the IALC for the opportunity afforded me. It is another golden opportunity to learn.
This kind of meeting has always being rewarding, refreshing,
and educative. I appreciate the endurance of Dr Paul Bradshaw
in his painstaking dealing with my many letters worrying him
about one thing or another. Bishop Colin Buchanan has been a
strong pillar to my education in liturgics; I run short of adequate
words to express my mind. He has been very marvellous. Rev.
Paul Gibson is another man I cannot forget in my life; he continues to give necessary assistance and encouragement. My host at
this meeting, Philip Tovey, is appreciated for his kindness to ac-
commodate free of cost. I am grateful to all of you and I love you
all and I say a big thank you. And I thank God who has made it
possible for me to attend this special meeting of the IALC.

Notes

1 For detailed discussion of Yoruba religious practice see J. Ọmọṣade
Awolalu, *Yoruba Beliefs and Sacrificial Rites* (London: Longman,
1979).

2 Judging from the expansion of Christianity in Yorubaland, it can be
said that the traditional religion is dying out gradually, but traditional
practices are still important forces among Yoruba people. See J. K. Parratt and A. R. I. Doi, 'Syncretism in Yorubaland', *Practical Anthropology* 15 (1969): 109–10.

3 E. Bolaji Idowu, *Olódumarè: God in Yoruba Belief* (London: Longmans, 1966), p. 108.

4 Sango was once the Oba of Oyo Empire who was feared during
his lifetime because of his power; see Awolalu, pp. 33–8; Idowu,
pp. 89–95; Modupe Oduyoye, 'The Sky: Lightning and Thunder', and
E. A. Adegbola, 'A Historical Study of Yoruba Religion', *Traditional
Religion in West Africa*, ed. E. A. Adegbola (Ibadan: Daystar Press,
1983), pp. 389–95, and 412–18; I. A. Akinjogbin and Biodun Adediran,
'Pre-colonial Nigeria: West of the Niger', *Nigerian History and Culture*,
ed. Richard Olaniyan (London: Longmans, 1985), pp. 39–40.

5 Oya was the wife of Sango and the goddess of River Niger; see
Idowu, pp. 91ff.

6 Egungun is worshipped in a form of venerating the spirits of the ancestors; see Janheinz Jahn, *Muntu: An Outline of the New African Culture*, trans. Marjorie Grene (London: Faber and Faber, 1961), pp. 70, 79.

7 Ogun cult is the cult of hunters, of soldiers, of all who deal in metal implements; see Idowu, pp. 85–89, 110f.

8 Anna Hinderer, *Seventeen Years in the Yoruba Country* (London: Religious Tract Society, 1877), p. 3.

9 John Mbiti, *Concepts of God in Africa* (London: SPCK, 1970), p. xiii.

10 A. E. Afigbo, 'Fact and Myth in Nigerian Historiography', *Traditional Religion in West Africa*, ed. Adegbola, p. 422.

11 Idowu, *Olódumarè*; Adegbola, 'Historical Study of Yoruba Religion'; Olaniyan, ed., *Nigerian History and Culture*; Awolalu, *Yoruba Beliefs*; E. A. Ayandele, *The Missionary Impact on Modern Nigeria, 1842–1914: A Political and Social Analysis* (London: Longmans, 1966).

12 Idowu, pp. 118–25; Awolalu, pp. 55–63.

13 Idowu, pp. 85–9, 110f.

14 Awolalu, p. 98.

15 See Awolalu and Ayandele.

16 Idowu, p. 108.

17 Ibid.

18 Ibid., p. 109.

19 Awolalu, p. 99.

20 Ibid.

21 Ibid., p. 100.

22 This ceremony was specifically observed on 17 July 2003 in Ondo town. Cf. Idowu, pp. 110f.

23 Awolalu, p. 101.

24 See Hugh Wybrew, *The Orthodox Liturgy* (Crestwood, NY: St Vladimir's Seminary Press, 1990), and elucidations provided by Dr Bert Breiner, supervisor on my doctoral thesis for the University of Birmingham (1988–90).

25 Awolalu, p. 102.

26 This is a kind of hymn common among all worshippers nowadays and is now adopted by the Christians during thanksgiving services such as harvest, new year, or Easter celebrations.

27 Idowu, p. 5.

28 J. O. Kayode and E. Dada Adelowo, 'Religions in Nigeria', *Nigerian History and Culture*, ed. Olaniyan, p. 233.

29 God is known particularly by this name, and he is also called Olorun with many attributes: Kayode and Adelowo, ibid., p. 235; cf. Mbiti, *Concepts of God in Africa*, p. 336. See full discussion of the name in Idowu, pp. 30ff.

30 Kayode and Adelowo, p. 234. For various kinds and purposes of sacrifice, see Idowu, pp. 118–25.

31 Kayode and Adelowo, p. 234.

32 Ibid., p. 236.

33 Ibid., p. 234.

34 See chapter 7 of the presenter's thesis for Birmingham University.

35 E. Bolaji Idowu, *Towards an Indigenous Church* (London: Oxford University Press, 1965), pp. 1–6.

36 See Chapter 6 of the presenter's thesis for further discussion on adaptation and indigenization.

37 Idowu, *Towards an Indigenous Church*, p. 5.

38 The undue 'marriage' of the Anglican Church of Nigeria to the Church of England and its traditions gives this impression.

39 Idowu, *Towards an Indigenous Church*, p. 6.

40 Ibid., p. 31.

41 Cited by C. O. Osun, 'Worship in Independent Churches: A Reflection', lecture presented to the Department of Mission, Selly Oak Colleges, Birmingham, England, 26 February 1990, p. 5.

42 Akin Euba, 'Music in Nigeria Today', *Nigerian History and Culture*, ed. Olaniyan, pp. 341–55, and sources there cited.

43 Music and songs are often used to relay messages, especially proverbial songs. This is common among hunters and professional drummers.

44 Idowu, *Olódùmarè*, pp. 113–15.

45 Wyatt Tee Walker, *Somebody's Calling My Name: Black Sacred Music and Social Change* (Valley Forge, PA: Judson Press, 1979), p. 17.

46 Ibid., p. 22.

47 Ibid., p. 23.

48 cf. Idowu, *Towards an Indigenous Church*, pp. 48–9.

49 Elizabeth McEwen Shields, *Music in the Religious Growth of Children* (New York: Abingdon-Cokesbury, 1943), p. 62.

50 John K. Parratt and Abdur Rahman I. Doi, 'Syncretism in Yorubaland: A Religious or Sociological Phenomenon?' *Practical Anthropology* 16 (1969): 105.

51 Michael Gelfand, *Medicine and Custom in Africa* (Edinburgh: E. & S. Livingstone, 1964), especially the first six chapters; Idowu, *Olódùmarè*, pp. 99, 106, 215.

52 Parratt and Doi, p. 254.

53 *Dictionary of the Apostolic Church* (New York: Charles Scribner's Sons, 1916), s. v. 'Ignatius of Antioch'.

54 *Liturgy of the Church of Nigeria (Anglican Communion): The Order for the Holy Communion of the Eucharist* (Ibadan, Nigeria: Ibadan University Press, 1983).

3

LITURGICAL FORMATION AND EDUCATION OF THE PEOPLE OF GOD[1]

Mark Earey

'Liturgical formation' – what do we mean?

The term 'liturgical formation' can be multi-layered, meaning different things to different people and in different contexts.

- It may mean formation *for* liturgy, in the sense of deepening people's understanding, answering questions such as 'Why?', 'What does this mean?', 'Where does this come from?' This aspect might equally well be called liturgical education.
- It is sometimes used to mean formation for those who *lead* liturgical worship, answering questions such as, 'How can it, or *should* it, be done?' We might think of this as liturgical training.
- It can be also mean the way that liturgical worship forms us, addressing underlying issues such as, 'What does this worship *do* to me or to us?' This is an essential requirement for true engagement with (or participation in) worship.

In practice these three different emphases can overlap and, indeed, they *ought* to overlap. For instance, understanding something about the roots (both historical and theological) of particular practices in worship can affect the way a service is led and should be part of the training of worship leaders. This in turn will (or ought to) have an effect on the shaping of God's people by worship.

In this chapter we focus particularly on the importance of education in liturgical formation and the implications this has for the way worshippers are formed in and by worship.

Education as part of formation

Sometimes liturgical 'education' seems to be nothing more than explaining or defending the 'exotic' or incomprehensible. It is tempting to conclude that it might be better to decide to omit from our worship things that require such explanations and save our energy for something more constructive. However, at the local church level and for the ordinary worshipper (certainly in the Church of England), such decisions to *change* worship are normally taken by other people, whether that is the minister, the worship committee, the church council, or the General Synod. Ordinary worshippers, in the short-term at least, often have to live *with* the 'exotic' or the opaque, but *understanding* can be the first step to engaging with it and maybe, ultimately, to fresh thinking.

For example, the most common question that I have been asked by ordinary worshippers throughout my ministry has been about the Nicene Creed. The question usually goes something like: 'Why do we say that we believe in one holy *catholic* Church? I thought we were Church of England.' It takes a very simple piece of explanation to bring about understanding, and such understanding can set the worshipper free to engage with the Creed rather than be tripped up by it.

Liturgical education can empower the people of God to question the *status quo* and to engage for themselves in new and creative thinking. It can give them criteria (including biblical criteria) by which to evaluate the words and rituals which form part of their worship. This sort of liturgical education is 'prophetic' rather than merely repressive instruction. It is education that is designed to set people free and to enable change, rather than to trap them in existing patterns. This is why it overlaps with the other understandings of the term 'liturgical formation'.

Liturgical education

Liturgical education is much easier to grasp and to talk about if one is considering the needs of those being trained for some kind of authorized ministry. One can talk about the syllabus, discuss teaching techniques, and ultimately require those concerned to undergo such education (though it is impossible, of course, to ensure *learning*).

For lay people, Christian education (including liturgical education) often ends after confirmation classes. If the confirmation classes are based on *Alpha* (as many are in the Church of England these days), then there may have been very little liturgical education at all.[2] Many congregations may have ongoing groups for Bible study and Christian nurture, but the corporate worship of the church is not often on the agenda of such groups or courses. This means that congregation members may have little opportunity to see the connections between what they discover in the Bible and the worship which forms and shapes them on Sundays.

An 86-year-old member of a congregation once told me that, as she had been coming to church all her life, she knew everything she needed and therefore didn't need to come to courses or groups of any sort. Developing the idea of lifelong Christian learning has a long way to go in many parts of the church.

There is among many ordinary worshippers (and leaders) a very low level of 'learner motivation'. As was discovered when *Common Worship* was being introduced, one of the best ways to overcome this is to bring out a new service book or in some other way to change the pattern of worship in a church. Even though people may resist the change itself, their awareness that change will affect them motivates them to learn and to understand.

Developing a strategy

One of the lessons learned during the changeover from the *Alternative Service Book 1980* (ASB) to *Common Worship* was that the most effective way to facilitate liturgical education for lay people was to provide assistance to clergy and lay leaders in local churches. The various *Praxis* training packs[3] were widely used at diocesan, deanery, and parish level. A key part of their success seemed to be that *Praxis* was a '*semi*-official' organization and therefore it didn't feel like 'Big Brother' telling people the right way to think. Though the internet was still in its infancy in England, churches were able to use it as a means of accessing materials.[4] This was particularly useful because it enabled 'leapfrogging' over clergy and so made materials and information available directly to lay people and lay leaders. The numbers of enquiries to *Praxis* from churchwardens, for instance, was very encouraging.

It is interesting that additional study materials which were produced 'centrally' did not have the same impact.[5] The production of these materials involved many of the same people who were working on the *Praxis* packs, and they encouraged worshippers to reflect on their existing experience of worship and to make connections with the new services being introduced. They were available for free, and one might have expected the take-up to be significant, but the opposite seemed to be the case.

All of this has implications for the current and commendable 'Transforming Worship' initiative of the Church of England's Liturgical Commission. The production of *Worship Changes Lives*[6] is a good example of an attempt at some flexible local-level education, designed to help worshippers to see the transformative potential in worship. An attractive full-colour booklet (backed up by a website, including resources for small groups), it is designed to be used in local churches to initiate discussion. Sales have been good, and no one can doubt the value of such an aim, but there are questions about whether, in the long-term, the Liturgical Commission are the people who can deliver this sort of liturgical education, for many of the reasons cited above. There can be a suspicion in many parts of the church of anything 'central', particularly among those who see anything liturgical as simply an exercise in control. The intention is that the Liturgical Commission works with partners, including diocesan liturgical committees, but the initiative is clearly coming from the 'centre' and that may be a long-term problem. Ultimately, without local 'demand', central 'supply' may not be able to bring about the transformation that is intended.

Partnership and pastoral connections

The strategies outlined above worked well when the 'new liturgy' was on its way (or, more importantly, when the old liturgy, the ASB, was no longer going to be an option). But what about when there is no new material and learner motivation among clergy and congregations is low? All the techniques and resources will still be valid, but the challenge will be how to reach beyond those for whom liturgy is already a particular interest. In a situation like this, the key to maintaining or commencing liturgical education for the whole people of God is the development of partnerships and connections.

Partnerships need to be developed between liturgy and other more 'fashionable' issues. That might include things such as Fresh Expressions, spirituality, or children's work. It means looking for anything that people *will* go to or *will* be motivated to learn about, and looking for ways of introducing liturgical education into those opportunities. If there is a training day on children's work, a workshop might be offered which makes links to worship. At a big event run by the diocesan spirituality group, it may be possible to be involved and to 'model' good and creative liturgical practice.

Connections need to be developed with other areas of local church life and pastoral practice. Where lay people are involved in marriage preparation, how can their training include a proper engagement with the marriage service and the shape of Christian marriage which is revealed and expressed in it? Or where lay people are involved in bereavement visiting, are they familiar with the funeral liturgy? Do they use prayers from it in pastoral visiting? Have they wrestled with the theology of death and eternal life which is given expression in the funeral service? Or maybe connections can be made between work with children and the liturgy of the church.

The biggest hindrance to liturgical education

But there remains one huge hindrance to liturgical education for the people of God, and it is, quite simply, that liturgy is largely seen as something about which there are 'right' and 'wrong' answers. This can make people feel intimidated, that they have little expertise, and that they may be exposed and vulnerable if they get it wrong. Those who would consider themselves 'professional' liturgists are often guilty of reinforcing this view, not least by the way that they talk about '*the* liturgy', as if it were a single monolithic 'thing'. Recent scholarship[7] should have made us very wary of speaking in such a way, as it has revealed how *little* we know about the origins and development of early Christian worship. It may be wiser to speak of 'liturgical worship' rather than of 'the liturgy'.

Many people seem to experience liturgical worship as something of which they are victims. This is why we should be interested in liturgical education which empowers, releases creativity, and banishes fear. It will be education which doesn't just teach facts but recognizes key principles, which bursts bubbles of false confidence, and which gives people a basic grammar of how worship 'works'.[8]

This sort of liturgical education for the people of God will not, of itself, produce good and deep liturgical formation (in its truest sense), but it can clear the way to make such formation more likely and more possible.

Liturgical formation

So we now turn to liturgical *formation* for the people of God – shaping people not just *for* worship but *by* worship. If worship is to form people for Christian living and for sharing in God's mission, there is a key question to address before all other questions: Is public worship seen to be *connected* with the rest of life, or an *escape* from the rest of life?

All of us will have experienced people using public worship as an escape from life. The classic Church of England 8.00 a.m. Prayer Book Communion service is an obvious example, where the quiet, the atmosphere, the Tudor English, so deliberately different from ordinary life, can make God feel closer for some people. Equally, one can see the same thing at work sometimes in a wild charismatic or Pentecostal praise service, or the ethereal beauty of Catholic ritual. There are times, of course, when such escape is important for the individuals concerned, but it is not the primary job of the church's public worship.

In the western world it often seems that the starting point for understanding worship is the personal relationship of the individual with God.

- 'Me and God' becomes the primary understanding of worship.
- Corporate worship is simply lots of people doing 'me and God' in the same building.
- 'Life' is what we have to go back to when we can't avoid it any longer.

It is disturbing that people still talk about worship as 'meeting with God' or that 'in worship we engage with God and encounter God' or that in worship we 'offer our lives to God'. This is only true if by 'worship' we mean the living of our whole lives to God's praise and glory. For Christians the primary place of engagement with God, encounter with God and offering to God is the day-to-day living of our lives for God, Monday to Saturday. It is the Spirit of God that produces encounter with God, and that Spirit is active in the world and in our lives, not merely in public worship. To associate this encounter solely with corporate worship is to risk losing the expectation that it can take place in any other context. We all need to recover a sense that the corporate gathering for worship on Sunday (which we might call 'liturgy', whether or not it takes a consciously liturgical form) is symbolic of this 'worship by living', a subset of the wider picture. Liturgy is therefore inseparable from life.

Though it is tempting to speak as if liturgical formation is a problem, the reality is that it is all too *easy*. Christians are constantly formed in their assumptions about God and about the Christian faith by their worship experience: it just 'happens'. The question is, what *sorts* of assumptions are being formed and what sort of Christian life is being shaped? The experience of talking to people about liturgical change is that many Church of England worshippers have been shaped by the dominance of the print medium and the book-focused culture which it fosters. The first question is generally, 'Why should we change?' rather than, 'Why haven't we changed more often?' For many Anglicans the assumption is that the norm for worship is that it is static and unchanging. This can, in turn, form a static view of God. This is formation of a sort, but perhaps we would be better calling it *de*-formation. It is, of course, possible to see liturgical formation work more positively.

During the first year of my ordination training I attended a non-Anglican church. It was an independent New Church (what we used to call a 'house church') which met in a converted carpet warehouse. It had a large (mainly young) congregation, lively worship and challenging preaching. I went because I knew it would be my last chance to experience, on a regular basis, worship which was different from the normal Anglican liturgical fare. I greatly enjoyed my involvement with the church but after a few months began to feel uneasy, sensing that something was missing. Eventually I realized what it was: intercession. The worship of this church regularly included confession (not in a formal liturgical sense, but often through song); there was sometimes prayer for healing for individuals; and often we prayed that our friends might come to share our Christian faith. What was missing was regular, consistent prayer for those in government, the nations of the world, for peace, for justice, for the poor and for the sick. I began to realize that my regular experience of intercession had formed my assumptions, not only about worship but about God. I realized that my strong beliefs about God's concern for justice (for instance) had come not from sermons but from hearing the regular prayers of the people in worship.

Of course, a culture of regular and insistent individual choice can also form or deform Christians. What sort of Christians are shaped by the assumption, for instance, that worship is a matter of choosing – menu-style – a particular service, or church, which suits our natural preferences, where we may engage primarily with people who share our background, personality, 'style', class, educational background, age, or gender?

From jigsaw to journey

So how can we aid a positive formation of the people of God through the worship experience? One simple way is to make sure that the shape of worship is clear and that worship can be seen as not just a *jigsaw puzzle* but a *journey*.

One of the most significant things about the *Common Worship* services is the emphasis on the shape, structure, and flow of services. An outline page at the beginning of each service shows its basic structure. The use of headings in the service itself reveals its shape – not just titles for individual elements (e.g., confession, Lord's Prayer) but section headings which reveal the overall shape and direction of the service (Gathering; Liturgy of the Word; Liturgy of the Sacrament; Sending Out). Of these, perhaps the most important to get right is that final section: Sending Out. The service should not just peter out or stop, but send us out, commissioned, strengthened, and shaped for living for God in our home, school, college, work, and leisure contexts.

When the *Common Worship* services came out, parishes were encouraged to use them flexibly and adapt them to their particular mission context. The texts were made available electronically to support this approach.[9] The result is that many parishes have produced their own service booklets.[10] Clergy frequently said to me that it was only when they came to produce their own booklets and looked at matters as simple and practical as headings and titles, that they saw for themselves the shape and flow of the Eucharist. Many had seen it as a jigsaw puzzle (in which the aim was to make sure that all the pieces were present) rather than as a journey (in which the aim is transformation). The same will be true for many worshippers. This is passive education, but it can spark questions, motivate learning, and be a tool for formation.

Engagement

One model for understanding liturgical worship is that of liturgy as a drama in which we 'play the Christian part' and are shaped thereby.[11] In the original television series of Star Trek, the part of Mr. Spock was played by the actor Leonard Nimoy. He says that after playing the part for many years, he found himself at home responding to members of his family 'in role', saying things like, 'But that's illogical . . .' If this sort of 'formation' can result from the very human experience of playing a part, how much more can Christians expect to be formed into the likeness of Christ through Spirit-filled worship.

It is the model of liturgy as drama which leads to my preference for the term 'engagement' rather than 'active participation'. Active participation can very soon sound as if we simply want people to do 'jobs' in church: to read the Bible, lead the prayers, or help distribute communion. Or it can suggest that we only 'participate' when we are speaking or singing.

'Engagement' is much broader and much deeper: we are 'engaged' when every part of our being, body, mind, and spirit, is taken up with what we are doing. We are engaged in worship when we know ourselves to be part of what is going on; in silence, in awe, in joy, in listening, in speaking, in moving, in sharing news. Sometimes what looks like worship as 'spectator-sport' (as it can sometimes appear to be in both cathedral evensong and large so-called mega-churches, for instance) can be experienced by the worshipper as more engaging than the self-conscious 'work of the people' which has been such a catchphrase of liturgical renewal for many decades and which sometimes results in little more than sharing liturgical jobs out among more people. This is important because to be *formed* and transformed by God through liturgical worship, one has to be engaged by it. In much the same way as even an 'extra', or a member of the chorus, in a film or a play has to remain in role and play their part in order for the whole performance to have authenticity, so in worship, whether we have named parts, 'speaking parts' or not, we all have a part to play. And there is no 'audience'—except God.

Recovering 'humanity' in liturgical worship

Here we come to the biggest problem with liturgical formation of the congregation: 'being part of it', being engaged, is not always how it feels. Those who are in charge, who make the decisions, sometimes make 'participation' feel as if it is a matter of doing the 'right' things in the 'right' way . . . and ordinary worshippers feel de-skilled.

In one parish in the 1980s, when modern services began to replace the Prayer Book at the main service, the congregation was taught to stand throughout the eucharistic prayer (where previously, during the Prayer Book 'consecration prayer' they had sat after the *Sanctus*). The theory was good: a greater sense of the unity of the prayer when the people stand confidently in the presence of God as a sign of corporate participation in the prayer. Eileen, a lady in her 80s, and many others in the congregation, simply experienced a sense of exclusion and alienation, as they found it physically difficult to stand for long periods. They felt that they were 'failing' (who?) if they sat down during the prayer.

Sometimes it is as if liturgy has lost its humanity and therefore those vital connections that reveal it as something which is part of a life lived to the glory of God. Liturgical worship needs to emphasize the connections with ordinary life, which make ritual natural, open, obvious ('naturally suggestive'), and in need of no special explanation. We may need to prune away some of the dead symbols which disconnect liturgy from life, and we need to make sure that liturgy does not exclude the very ordinary human elements of humour and storytelling.

In many churches children take part in their own separate learning and worship activities and join the adult congregation towards the end of the service. Often they are encouraged to share what they have learned or made or discovered about God. After the children have shared what they have discovered about God, why not ask adults what they want to share with others about what God has said to them, what they've felt or been reminded of, or what they have heard afresh? This is not simply reflection on the sermon or learning; it is, rather, an opportunity to reflect on the whole experience of worship and to share their stories with one another. There is, of course, a huge risk in this sort of approach. There is a lack of control. There is the possibility that someone will say something offensive, inappropriate, or just plain daft. But this is itself formational—the Christian life is one of risk, of handing over control and learning to trust God. It is good when this is given expression in public worship.

Final remarks

If connections and partnership are important principles and tools for the liturgical *education* of the people of God, then they are also vital for the *formation* of the people of God. The Christian life is one lived in tension between the 'now' and the 'not yet': between our current experience and the fullness of the reign of God. Christian liturgy should energize and symbolize that tension, not by bridging the gap in a static way but by drawing the two together, rather like elastic, so that the 'now' is constantly drawn towards the 'not yet'.

For this to work, for the tension to be constructive and creative, the elastic must be attached at both ends. Worship *will* form us and shape our assumptions about God, whether for good or bad – formation or *de*formation. Worship which is in spirit and truth will be authentic both to who God is and to where we are.

Notes

1 In its original form for the IALC 2003, this paper was a reflection on liturgical formation in the light of the Church of England's relatively recent experience of introducing the new *Common Worship* services. The author had during that period been National Education Officer for Praxis, an organization for liturgical renewal and education, and had played a role in that process. In its current (significantly revised and updated) form it has been published in Mark Earey and Phillip Tovey, *Liturgical Inculturation and Common Worship* (Cambridge: Grove Books, 2009). It is reproduced here (slightly amended) with permission.

2 The *Alpha* course deliberately steers clear of topics which are denominationally controversial (such as baptism and holy communion) in order to make it ecumenically hospitable. This policy may be wise in itself, but it means that liturgical matters, which are central to the experience of worship in most Church of England contexts, are absent and will need tackling in other ways.

3 Praxis training packs covered most of the particular elements of *Common Worship* (such as Holy Communion, lectionary, pastoral services and initiation) as well as the process of 'making the change' itself. They were published privately by Sarum College Bookshop, Salisbury.

4 There was a Praxis section on the Sarum College website and colour versions of the Praxis packs were available for download.

5 *Getting to Know Common Worship: Material to help with the introduction of Common Worship at the local level* (London: Church House Publishing, 2000). This was produced by the Education and Communication sub-group of the Liturgical Publishing Group. It was also made freely available on the *Common Worship* website.

6 Paul Bradshaw and Peter Moger, eds, *Worship Changes Lives: How it Works, Why it Matters* (London: Church House Publishing, 2008).

7 For instance, Paul Bradshaw, *The Search for the Origins of Christian Worship* (2nd edn, London: SPCK, 2002).

8 See Mark Earey, *Liturgical Worship: A Fresh Look – How it Works; Why it Matters* (London: Church House Publishing, 2002) for a book which includes some theology and history of Christian worship, but is primarily about the basic principles underlying liturgical worship.

9 *Common Worship* texts are available through the *Visual Liturgy Live* software (www.visualliturgylive.net) or for free download as RTF files from the Church of England website (www.cofe.anglican.org).

10 See Mark Earey, *Producing Your Own Orders of Service* (London: Church House Publishing/Praxis, 2000), which gives guidance about liturgical principles as well as practical design and production issues.

11 For more on this, see Mark Earey, *Worship as Drama*, Grove Worship Series 140 (Cambridge: Grove Books, 1997).

4

THE ROLE OF MUSIC IN LITURGICAL FORMATION

Carol Doran

'The world is charged with the grandeur of God,' wrote the Victorian mystic poet Gerard Manley Hopkins. Many people tell us that such grandeur is a path by which they are drawn closer to God.

This chapter will explore another, related path toward God. It is the way of communal prayer. Some people are methodically taught to take their appropriate place in established liturgical practice. Others learn by osmosis or discover accidentally the ways liturgy can transform their perceptions of holy scripture and the traditions that inform our faith.

The word 'liturgy' is thought by many to include music as an integral component. In this paper music will be examined in terms of its unique role in liturgical formation. We will consider both the several ways that the faithful are formed by it to participate authentically in the church's liturgies and how, through that participation, they may be awakened to greater love of God.

The essential thesis of this presentation is that music, because of its inherent nature – its beauty and its rhythmic patterns –

draws both the stranger and the faithful toward the Church's liturgical prayer. Music symbolically communicates its meaning and encourages increasingly deeper participation in it. In offering this discussion, I urge consideration of an additional matter that concerns many liturgical leaders today: what element, presently absent from our liturgical practice, would enable the unique potential music possesses to be more fully utilized in the church's liturgical life, so that its total mission, including hospitality and evangelism, will be strengthened and enriched?

The inherent nature of music draws people to it

Recent research in neuroscience reports with increasing clarity that all humans are, and have been from earliest human history, makers of music.[1] In his book *The Art Instinct: Beauty, Pleasure, and Human Evolution,* Denis Dutton describes music as

> one of the supreme art forms: universal across cultures and history, a focus of spontaneous interest from infancy, and for many individuals a source of consuming, lifelong pleasure. All this despite the fact that the ability to perceive its medium – pitched sound – has almost no imaginable significance for survival in natural selection.[2]

The nature of music is inherently attractive, even to people who describe themselves as deaf. When congregations of deaf people incorporate instruments like drums into their worship rituals, the drums' vibrations travel through the floor and the furniture in the worship space. The people experience those vibrations through the sensory receptors in their skin.

The remarkable trans-cultural studies of the neuro-physiologist Dr Manfred Clynes were among an early wave of 'brain-science' work that has drawn increasing interest in the twenty-first century. His book *Sentics* (published in 1989) reported evidence that human beings living in all parts of the world, no matter what their cultural experience has been, perceive strongly consistent emotional meanings in music played for them during hundreds of field tests.[3]

This ability to communicate cross-culturally might be thought of as music's 'Pentecost' quality. People singing in their own culture's musical expression are able to be understood at some level by all. The present popularity of 'world music' in the wider culture and in congregational singing in the churches gives evidence of this phenomenon.

Experienced liturgical/musical leaders are not surprised when they encounter resistance to the idea of singing unfamiliar musical styles and learning texts in languages other than the one spoken by most of the people in the congregation. But many have learned to use music's ability to win hearts and minds in the process of introducing the unfamiliar. Teaching, encouraging, and singing beautiful new music from a distant culture often eliminates the need to debate the relative value of each style. The same quality of music that builds community has the capability to reconcile us to one another. In the act of creating something beautiful with others, the need to convince them of the value of one's own musical preferences tends to evaporate.

From this perspective, we are being formed for liturgy when we sing together. When we listen to one another's singing in order to blend our voices and to produce a rhythmic unity, we are expressing respect for others and reconciling the variety of musical experiences, understanding, and preferences present within the group. In our liturgical music-making we express our theology.

Archbishop Rowan Williams has said, 'We have to learn to be human alongside all sorts of others, the ones whose company we don't greatly like, whom we didn't choose, because Jesus is drawing us together into his place, his company.'[4]

Another of music's valuable contributions to liturgical formation is its ability to participate in revelation – to encourage people's awareness of the presence of the living God.

The reclaiming of this quality in church music during the 1960s was strongly influential in establishing the importance of music's role in that era's liturgical renewal. When texts about God's transcendent wonder were sung to familiar tunes from people's daily lives, many exuberantly celebrated the concept of 'God among us', even though they had never pronounced or even understood the meaning of the words 'immanence' or 'transcendence'.

Music, together with other arts, is able to spark the imagination. It is able to take our thinking beyond the rational and logical modes. Janet Walton has identified music's ability to create 'illusion' – that quality of art 'that reaches beyond the bounds of tangible realities'.[5]

'The purpose of art is not the imitation of reality. Rather, art is created to express "otherness" or illusion.'[6]

Isadora Duncan, one of the great dancers of the twentieth century, describes it this way:

> This is what we are trying to accomplish: to blend together a poem, a melody and a dance, so that you will not listen to the music, see the dance or hear the poem, but will live in the scene and the thought that all are expressing.[7]

Many of the guitar players and singers who became leaders of liturgical music during the 1960s shared Duncan's goals: that people will be praying in the holy reality created by the combined liturgical text, music, and ritual.

Music, because it is a mystery itself, reminds us that God is a mystery. People interviewed in a study by Robert Wuthnow of Princeton University describe being moved by divine beauty while listening to music, or feeling awed by the realization that holy mysteries are beyond comprehension. Participants said that they believe the arts (including music) release in them creative energies that allow them to reflect more deeply on God.[8]

As tempting as it may be to dismiss such comments as expressions of the character of the time and the culture in which they were made, we could do so only if we were willing also to toss out with them the works of some of our tradition's greatest writers. Who is this mysterious 'Love' George Herbert describes as divinely forgiving and welcoming in his text 'Love bade me Welcome'? Like the people interviewed for Wuthnow's twenty-first-century study, this great seventeenth-century poet knew the power of God's mystery to intrigue and fascinate. If Herbert had written instead an empirical account of our Lord's actions at that meal, would that writing provide the same spiritual nourishment and joy four centuries later?

Perhaps music's most important role in liturgy is to increase the worshipper's understanding of the meaning of texts that are sung. While not the same as spoken and written language, music itself is a complex symbol system of vibratory patterns that, in its own way, is able to communicate meaning. Perhaps no musician we know was more imaginative in the use of this potential than Johann Sebastian Bach. His use of specific melodic patterns to intensify the listeners' perception of the text was brilliantly conceived. His music is able to communicate effectively, even to those living three centuries later, such concepts as sadness (by means of a series of descending half-steps), hope (by a series of rising whole-steps), jubilation (using bright major tonalities), inevitability (bass instrument or voice moving downward in half-steps), and many other emotions.

Although Bach's use of this technique, sometimes called 'text painting', was far more artistically successful than similar efforts by his contemporaries, text painting was a common practice in the eighteenth century, and the church benefited greatly from it.

Ambivalence about the nature of music has clouded its potential to benefit the Church

The Judeo-Christian tradition includes accounts of music's presence in worship throughout its history. The Hebrew Bible describes a people singing, dancing, and playing musical instruments in praise of God. In 2 Chronicles, God's overwhelming presence experienced in the midst of music is dramatically recorded in this account of the liturgy at the dedication of Solomon's great temple:

It was the duty of the trumpeters and singers to make themselves heard in unison in praise and thanksgiving to the LORD, and when the song was raised, with trumpets and cymbals and other musical instruments, in praise to the LORD . . . the house, the house of the LORD, was filled with a cloud, so that the priests could not stand to minister because of the cloud; for the glory of the LORD filled the house of God. (2 Chron. 5.13–14, NRSU)

But the New Testament carries no parallel record of such extravagant musical ensembles. Even though many of the earliest Christians had been formed through Jewish ritual and prayer, they intended to differentiate themselves from Roman orgiastic cults which used musical instruments to encourage their revelry.

The early Christians sang (unaccompanied) psalms and hymns and spiritual songs to God.[9] In the letter to the Ephesians, their singing is associated with being filled with the Holy Spirit. In Colossians, music is used not only to teach but to admonish one another. The young church in hiding risked the lives of its members by singing together. Who might hear their voices and report their illegal gathering? Who might overhear individuals singing hymns to Christ while going about their daily work?

And yet, the benefits to the church that are inherent to music were known and valued so highly from the church's earliest days that even severe persecution did not stop the church's singing. Rick Fabian has offered a larger perspective or the historical pattern of the early church's use of music:

The most powerful tool for Church reform is music. Each previous reform has brought a new infusion of music into the Church's life, conveying the reforming ideals into the hearts of church folk, and drawing unchurched people in great numbers into the new movement. . . . No means [other than music] could be more effective for uniting the churches in a common mission to tell the world about our common life in Christ.[10]

By the beginning of the fifth century, Augustine of Hippo records his concerns about the ability of music sung during the liturgy to fascinate and to draw the mind and emotions both toward and away from the text being sung. He wrestles intellectually with the problem of sin which he perceives to be occurring when the listener enjoys hearing the music.

The soul of this wise and faithful man is deeply conflicted by the question of music's appropriate place in liturgy. Augustine knows that music is beautiful; he remembers that the beauty of music was active in drawing him toward the church at an earlier time. He knows that music has a role in building up the church. Augustine speaks of the way God's truths are received into him on the wings of beautiful music. He writes that those truths kindle a flame of piety in his mind more when they are sung than if they are merely spoken. Augustine does not question whether faithful people benefit from music; he knows that they do, even though he seems to consider singing in church to be a concession to 'weaker minds' who need special treats to arouse their devotion.

Augustine is filled with guilt when he finds himself enjoying music. Unfortunately, this happens to him even when he strongly intends to be unaffected by the music and only to pay attention to the words being sung. He sees 'reason' as the proper leader of prayer and believes that the 'bodily sense' is intended to aid reason, 'following after it in proper order'. Music, by taking a leading role, in Augustine's mind becomes an unruly associate.

This saint, although he claims he can 'depart' from the beauty of music when he chooses, realizes, in fact, that he cannot do so. He even considers recommending the banishment of psalm-singing from the church as one means of solving the problem of human temptation. And his inability to control music's effect on him is made doubly painful by his inability to explain why.

Planning to use music in liturgical formation

Is it possible to look at a centuries-old liturgical participant like music with an openness that expects fresh new meanings and results? It will be important to set aside the ways that have become listless through lack of attention and misuse, and to imagine, with the help of reasonable optimism, all that might be.

Catechesis is needed. Local parishes as well as seminaries often assume that liturgical practice and traditions of history and music are things 'everyone knows'. The 1992 report to the House of Bishops of the General Synod of the Church of England on theological training[11] reflects a situation in England not unlike the present situation in the eleven Episcopal seminaries in the United States. Although all eleven seminaries have programmes of regular corporate worship, there is no curricular plan for liturgical formation that is consistent throughout the country.

Formation for liturgy has not emerged as a primary focus in our post-modern society, either in seminaries or in individual parishes. However, where the faithful have been welcomed into the fullness of liturgical practice, including music, text, movement, drama, space, and visual arts, the resulting health of the community gives compelling proof of the value of such a programme of formation.

New hymnody has introduced refreshed language and exceeded the boundaries of long-established criteria. The remarkable hymn 'Will you come and follow me', from the Community at Iona in Scotland, for example, speaks to us in the voice of Christ. Not at all a text of 'praise', this hymn challenges us to consider our individual commitment to Christ's mission. 'Will you kiss the leper clean and do such as this unseen?' is one line of this text. In the final stanza, the church sings back in its own voice: 'Lord, your summons follows true when you but call my name. I will come and follow you and never be the same.'[12]

Change can be exhilarating, but when it is liturgical/musical change, careful preparation, continuing catechesis, and clergy–musician collaboration are essential. James Empereur, a Jesuit priest who acknowledges the role of ambiguity in a reconciling liturgical ministry, explains

A change in form will also mean a change in belief. It is not simply that we all believe the same about the resurrection of Christ and that we can then engage in different forms of the Easter Vigil. Rather, it is that all of us standing around the same Easter candle singing our paschal praises may well have divergent beliefs about what the resurrection of Christ means. Although we cannot fully agree about the resurrection of Christ on the discursive, rational self-autonomous level, we can enter into the same symbol because it addresses us more completely, and it is not limited to speaking to only our rationality.[13]

The surrounding culture has provided its own challenges to music's effective functioning in and for the church. Cuts in school budgets often affect the arts first. It has been decades since music reading has been taught in most state schools. As a result, many people living in western cultures today believe that the term 'music maker' could never be applied to them. The ubiquity of recordings of confident singers only reminds us of the vast gulf we believe exists between the performer's musical gifts and the sound of our own voices. 'I can't sing,' people often say, just before they relate a still-painful story of their fourth-grade teacher telling them to 'just mouth the words' while the rest of the class sings a song during the time of parents' visitation.

In John L. Bell's wonderful book *The Singing Thing*, he writes about communities all across the globe, from eastern Europe to sub-Saharan Africa, in which singing is 'a natural thing' that everyone does together. He describes working with people who sing 'three to five-part harmonies of hundreds of songs which they have learned by ingestion rather than by instruction'.[14]

From his experience Bell knows that such communal singing is possible when we 'believe in [our] voices' and in '[our] ability to recall instantly melodies and harmonies' we have learned.[15] When we consciously choose to sing rather than to evaluate our ability to do so, and when we recognize that singing in church is at least as much fun as karaoke, we will have chosen the better way. This is not a complicated task, but it is critically important that we regularly practise it with our young children.

The role of the musical leader of liturgy

Although singing is a natural human activity, organizing singing in liturgy usually is the responsibility of someone or some group of people. Without systematic encouragement, a congregation is unlikely to be aware of the traditional expectation that those who know God will automatically sing God's praises. Congregational singing often is thought of as an 'option' – something I may do 'if I feel like it' – rather than my joyful contribution to the community's corporate praise. The Catechism in the Book of Common Prayer of the Episcopal Church describes one aspect of the ministry of the laity as taking their place in the worship of the Church.[16] Those who find themselves even one time in the midst of a congregation that is singing together with palpable energy and joy usually do not forget the experience. When leaders draw people into enthusiastic participation in corporate praise, they are building up the community of faith.

Musical leaders of liturgy are both ordained and lay people who are led and encouraged to develop their musical gifts through work with expert teachers and personal investment in diligent practice of their craft. The co-ordination of these music ministries in the leadership of the congregation's music is a work of art in itself. Encouraging people to claim their ability to sing, for example, is doubly effective if two orders of ministry carry it out through both sermons and catechesis.

One of the most important tasks of the combined ordained/lay music leadership is to provide encouragement in the varieties of musical expression appropriate for use by Anglican communities at worship. Music and the texts it carries have ability to increase the breadth of people's perceptions about God and to transform them through liturgical experience. But often people assume that liturgical music has the same function as music they enjoy outside church. It is perceived as 'refreshment' between sections of spoken language in liturgy or as 'entertainment'.

Clergy who are prepared to work with the parish musician to explain liturgical choices and teach new music will be grateful to be able to draw from the skills that make up their own strong formation in music. Where such formation was not provided during seminary, work with knowledgeable musical and clerical colleagues can systematically fill the gap in professional preparation.

The model of the Cambridge Ecclesiologists should warm hearts and encourage independent study. These men were part of the 'second wave' of the Oxford Movement in England; they were active from 1839 to 1862. Having come to the conclusion by means of their own study and deliberation that congregational singing was an important element in building up the churches, this group of clergy and seminarians discovered that neither Oxford nor Cambridge Universities would respond to their requests for music education. So they found music teachers for themselves and went on to demonstrate effectively the validity of their assumptions about music's ability to revitalize liturgy.

Possibly the most unfortunate aspect of seminarians not having an opportunity to claim their vocal potential by becoming confident and skilful in singing is that those who do not see themselves as confident leaders of the congregation's music are unlikely to be advocates for it either.

An important aspect of clergy music leadership is intentionally developing respect for, and a healthy working relationship with, their colleagues in music ministry. Herein lies opportunity for the living-out of justice and reconciliation in the midst of the gathered people of God.

Imagining musical formation for liturgy

Imagine a parish where catechesis for children includes learning their congregation's musical settings of the ordinary and hymn-tunes they will take with them into their adult life in the church. When Martin Luther did this with new music for the Reformation church in Germany, the adults naturally sang along with their children's music-making at home and in the churches.

Imagine a parish where all choirs (children's and adults') integrated liturgical catechesis into every rehearsal and prayers before and after rehearsal. More than forty years ago, the choir at the cathedral in Seattle, Washington, decided to sing Compline at the end of each evening rehearsal. Because it was so moving to the singers, they invited their families to join their prayer. Eventually they decided to offer it to the cathedral and to the city every Sunday night. The practice continues to this day.

Imagine a meeting of the vestry that approves funds for the musician's continuing education in liturgy and the clergy's continuing education in music. Leadership models are changing. New information will be helpful.

Imagine a parish where settings of texts sung by the congregation are carefully chosen to express and enhance each ritual moment, where every liturgy's congregational song includes ancient and contemporary texts drawn from a worldwide collection and led creatively, respectfully, and with enthusiasm.

This closing comment about liturgy and art comes from Janet Walton's excellent book *Art and Worship*:

> We come [to liturgies] not to be entertained, though that may happen, but to engage in praise and thanksgiving, to gain insight, to gather strength and to express community in relationship with others. Art [including music] enables a community to feel these intangible experiences, to discover some aspects of God's ways of interacting, and to see connections with our everyday lives.[17]

Notes

1 See Steven Mithen, *The Singing Neanderthals: The Origins of Music, Language, Mind, and Body* (Cambridge, MA: Harvard University Press, 2006); Daniel J. Levitin, *This Is Your Brain on Music: The Science of a Human Obsession* (New York: Dutton, 2006); Andrew Newberg, Eugene D'Aquill and Vince Rause, *Why God Won't Go Away* (New York: Ballantine Books, 2001).

2 Denis Dutton, *The Art Instinct: Beauty, Pleasure, and Human Evolution* (New York: Bloomsbury Press, 2009), p. 212.

3 Manfred Clynes, *Sentics: The Touch of the Emotions* (rev. ed., Dorset, UK: Prism Press, 1989).

4 Rowan Williams, Enthronement Sermon, 27 February 2003, http://www.anglicancommunion.org/acns/news.cfm/2003/2/27/ACNS3328; accessed 25/07/09.

5 Janet Walton, *Art and Worship* (Wilmington, DE: Michael Glazier, 1988), p. 77.

6 Ibid.

7 Walton, quoting from *Isadora Speaks*, by Isadora Duncan, ed. Franklin Rosemont (San Francisco: City Light Books, 1981), p. 50.

8 Robert Wuthnow, *All in Sync: How Music and Art Are Revitalizing American Religion* (Berkeley and Los Angeles, CA: University of California Press, 2003), p. 238.

9 Ephesians 5.18–19, Colossians 3.16.

10 R. G. Fabian, 'Plan for the Mission of St Gregory of Nyssa' (December 1977), http:www.saintgregorys.org; accessed 2003.

11 The Steering Group for Theological Courses and The Advisory Group on Full-Time Theological Training, 'Theological Training: A Way Ahead: A Report to the House of Bishops of the General Synod of the Church of England' (London: Church House Publishing, 1992).

12 'Will you come and follow me', *Wonder, Love and Praise* (New York: Church Publishing, 1997), number 757.

13 James L. Empereur, SJ, 'How Can the Church Worship in Postmodern Times?', *Postmodern Worship and the Arts*, eds Doug Adams and Michael E. Moynahan, SJ (San Jose, CA: Resource Publications, 2002), p. 174.

14 John L. Bell, *The Singing Thing: A Case for Congregational Song* (Chicago: GIA Publications, 2000), p. 15.

15 Ibid., p. 16.

16 The Book of Common Prayer (New York: Church Hymnal Corp., 1979), p. 855.

17 Walton, p. 119.

5

LITURGICAL EDUCATION, TRAINING, AND FORMATION FOR ORDINANDS

Tomas S. Maddela

With the recovery of a baptismal ecclesiology and the recent liturgical reforms in many provinces of the Anglican Communion, Anglicans have restored the proper place of every baptized member of the church in its liturgy. Indeed we insist that by reason of the sacrament of baptism, every person is a member of the priestly people and has the right and duty to share in the liturgy. This, of course, goes beyond just delivering church members from being passive observers to taking more active roles.

But, while it is the *ekklesia*, the liturgical assembly of the local church, that celebrates the liturgy, there is in the assembly a variety of roles and degrees of participation. Daniel B. Stevick states it quite succinctly, 'Although the worshiping unit is the whole people, it is not an undifferentiated community. There are liturgical leaders, who act according to gift, training and appointment. But they act for all and in relation to all.'[1] Indeed, the mode of participation of people differs according to their liturgical competence, which has been often subject to development in the course of liturgical history and according to the needs of the local churches. But whether presidential roles increase or decrease, every liturgical assembly must have a president whose particular role is determined by the nature of the celebration as indicated in the rubrics.[2]

Most Books of Common Prayer continue to present numerous challenges to all liturgical participants but especially to those assigned to lead. [3] In this paper, we shall be focusing on ordinands. After all, upon them will eventually fall the role and obligation 'to ensure that the atmosphere in which the liturgy is celebrated is one that will not impede awareness of the presence of God, an atmosphere that will allow the Word of God to be heard with understanding, and, most importantly, an atmosphere that will allow the sacramental action to work clearly and directly while at the same time acknowledging the mystery, the presence of "the Other" in our worship'.[4] Perhaps it is too much to say – yet it should be considered – that the one presiding at any liturgical assembly who does not perform effectively and cannot relate with the rest of the assembly is wasting his/her time at the chancel and is also wasting the time of the participants whom s/he uniquely represents in the celebration.

Describing the situation in the Roman Catholic Church, Nathan Mitchell observed that 'within the Roman Catholic communion, the group in greatest need of liturgical education is the clergy. The comment is perhaps facetious, perhaps patronizing, but it surely expresses the doubt some Catholics have about the clergy's ability to preside effectively at public prayer. Vanished are the days an ordained minister's ritual competence was unquestionable; today's presiders are rated, berated, and sometimes (as happened recently in a California parish) assaulted.'[5] Although I haven't heard yet of an Anglican cleric being assaulted for reason involving presidency in the liturgy, the situation Mitchell observed is, I believe, also true in Anglican churches.

Nevertheless, there is also, in the worldwide Anglican Communion today, an earnest desire to provide the necessary preparation for candidates for ordination so that they become 'at home' with the Book of Common Prayer and effective in the performance of their roles as liturgical leaders and animators. This paper seeks to describe the elements that should normally be part of such preparation and some of the attendant issues or problems arising therefrom. In working this out, I am governed by certain frameworks which I wish to clarify beforehand:

1   Preparing ordinands for liturgical leadership involves a dynamic combination of *education, training,* and *formation.* As used in this paper, education refers to the imparting of the 'classics of liturgical studies' or the body of knowledge necessary for the subject to become thoroughly familiar with the various aspects of Christian worship, which includes, but is not limited to, its historical development, theology, pastoral dimensions, spirituality, structure and content, and even its juridical aspect.[6] Training refers to the variety of activities designed to enable the subject to acquire or hone skills in the crafting of a good liturgical celebration, including, but not limited to, conducting worship, preaching, reading, and liturgical musicianship. Formation refers to all other activities designed to imbue the subject with *an authentic liturgical power and spirit.*[7] The combination of these three elements is requisite for a wholistic/holistic preparation for liturgical leadership.

2   Although the seminary may not be the proper locus where such education, training, and formation may take place, in this paper, it is the seminary model that I use heavily. Some may object to this and therefore I beg for your indulgence. Indeed, the seminary as a setting for preparation for ordained ministry in general is under fire from many camps today, and the jury is still out as to its effectiveness in providing the requisite preparation for liturgical leadership. But it is from that context that I can speak with confidence buttressed by twenty-one years of being a seminary teacher, trainer, and formator of numerous men and women who now serve in both the Philippine Independent Church and the Episcopal Church in the Philippines. I must confess

that in preparing this paper, I have always kept our seminary in mind. Notwithstanding, in the latter part of this paper, I will raise the issue as to whether the seminary is indeed the proper place for the education, training, and formation of liturgical leaders.

3 In dealing with the question of how within the normal seminary programme we should we go about preparing candidates for ordination who will undertake central liturgical leadership in the church today, one would expect to give due consideration to the profile of those entering seminaries today. Important as that may be, I steer away from it for lack of adequate time and space. I take cognizance, however, that while seminarians form a seemingly homogenous group, their overall background is widely diverse. I have also been made aware that there have been, in recent years, radical changes in the profile of seminarians in almost all Provinces of the Anglican Communion.

Liturgical education for ordinands

There are two basic and distinct aspects of liturgical education. In the first place, the liturgy is in itself formative, didactic, and instructive.[8] On the other hand, there is a sense in which the liturgy is learned. While we are primarily concerned here with the second aspect, a brief outline of the first would also be helpful for our purpose.

If the liturgy is the 'primary and indispensable source of the true Christian spirit' for all, then surely its role in the formation of the ordinand is paramount in importance. In fact, there was a time when the church depended entirely on the liturgy for the formation of her faithful and even her priests. Josef Jungmann has established that during the first few centuries of the church's history the sacred liturgy was the only means of instruction.[9] The educative function of the liturgy was beautifully expressed by Pope Pius XI in his encyclical *Quas primas*:

The annual celebration of the sacred mysteries is more effective in instilling into the people the truths of faith and in bringing them the joys of the spiritual life than any pronouncements, however important, of the teaching Church. These appeal only to learned people but once, and then to the intellect, whereas the Church's feasts, which move and teach everyone, go on every year and forever and influence not only the mind but also the heart and the whole person. Since man is composed of body and soul, he needs to be aroused by the outward solemnities of the liturgy, in order that through the variety and beauty of the sacred ceremonies he can receive more abundantly the divine teachings into his soul, make them one with his own substance and blood, and thus use them to advance in the spiritual life.[10]

This does not mean in any way that the liturgy is the sole teaching force in the church, but rather that it is the principal and central source of Christian formation to which all other didactic efforts in the church should be related. Nor does it mean in the least that the liturgy should be turned into any kind of classroom experience or formal instruction. The liturgy teaches through its celebration and through signs, words, actions, and material things, by which it expresses the worship of God and the sanctification of God's people.[11]

Preparing people for liturgical leadership requires a more deliberate programme of instruction on the various aspects of the liturgy, which takes place mainly within an academic community and which relies mainly on modern scholarship.[12] Here we note that the scientific study of liturgy in seminaries is a relatively recent development.[13] Likewise, the number of schools or institutes which offer graduate degrees with specialization in liturgy for those who are to teach in the seminaries since the establishment of the Paris Institut Supérieur de Liturgie in 1956 can still be counted with the fingers of one's hands. Many will perhaps recall those years when the teaching of liturgy in seminaries or schools of theology was largely given by historians or systematic theologians.[14] We can be grateful today that in most seminaries, liturgical studies are, for the most part, handled by liturgists.[15]

James F. White asks whether it is possible to develop minimal expectations for a seminary in the teaching of worship. It is clear that only very flexible standards can be developed because there is such a variety in the denominations and types of schools involved. Yet some minimal expectations can be stated for the purpose of discussion and to help some schools to rise to them and others to go above them.[16]

It is indeed amazing the amount of convergence we now recognize on what all ministerial students need to know. Liturgical courses at the seminary level generally combine the historical, theological, and pastoral studies of the sacraments and other rites of the church.[17] In many seminaries, all undergraduate students have to take what is called 'core courses' and may choose from various elective offerings. Core courses typically include such offerings as 'General Introduction to the Liturgy and Sacraments'; 'The Eucharist'; 'The Sacraments of Initiation' or 'Rites of Passage'; 'The Liturgical Year'; 'The Divine Offices'; 'The Pastoral Offices (Marriage, Ministry to the Sick, Reconciliation, Burial Rites, and Blessings)'; and 'Homiletics'.

It is in the area of elective courses where seminaries differ largely. There is also a wider range of course offerings than can be tackled within the core courses. In some cases the offerings are extensive enough to include special courses in the liturgical traditions of other religious communions. Others offer studies in more specialized areas of interest such as 'liturgical arts', 'sanctification of time', 'the eucharistic prayer', 'liturgical inculturation' and 'Protestant liturgical renewal'. Still others offer the possibility of studying the anthropological roots of ritual and symbolism in greater depth.

There are several attendant issues/problems in relation to our search for an ideal form of liturgical education for ordinands. I proceed to point out some major ones:

1 A common problem plaguing seminaries and other institutions is how to integrate the study of liturgy with other ar-

eas of theological studies (biblical studies, systematics, spirituality, etc.). A number of schools have attempted to meet this need for greater co-ordination/integration through a method of 'team teaching' or through 'interdisciplinary studies'.[18] A related issue here involves clarifying the liturgical aspects of other disciplines. This can only come as other faculty members explore these dimensions in their work and when liturgical scholars likewise become more knowledgeable about other fields. James F. White correctly observes that what is happening today is that 'aspects of ministry are usually taught in watertight compartments and then students are expected to combine them all in ministry. Yet, the faculty cannot even talk to each other intelligently about each other's disciplines. But those bridges must be built so students can see worship as an integral part of all their entire work of ministry.'[19]

2 Another problem confronting many seminaries today concerns the academic training of those who teach liturgy. Ideally, of course, theological faculties must include people who are specially trained to teach Christian worship. The growth of liturgiology as a discipline, the increasing number of students studying it, the profound changes which have occurred in worship practice and style in the parishes, and the recognition of the importance of liturgical study in the seminary curriculum suggest that the time has come to staff liturgics courses in the seminaries with credentialed teachers. These are people who are most likely to connect the theoretical and practical aspects of worship because those aspects are held together in their own academic training and pastoral experience. But the number of schools offering this kind of training is not always accessible and many seminaries are in dire financial straits to provide for the appropriate training of a person as part of faculty development.

3 A third problem concerns the library and other resources available to support the liturgical education programmes of seminaries. There are numerous liturgical resources now

available to open students to the treasury of liturgical data for their studies. They even come in various media forms (CDs, VCDs/DVDs, maps, and even the Internet). Many seminary libraries, however, especially in the so-called 'third-world countries', do not have ready access to them or simply cannot afford them. Much also depends on who are handling the liturgy courses and who prioritizes library acquisitions.

Liturgical training of ordinands

One factor that makes teaching liturgy truly delightful is that it is in this area, more than in any other, where theory and practice are closely combined. Indeed, many seminaries provide more deliberate training programmes or 'practica' to enable students to acquire skills or hone what they already possess for more effective liturgical leadership. It is also in this area where liturgy professors are constantly challenged to take more cognizance of the kind of liturgical leadership that is expected of ordinands when they are finally fielded. Some seminaries even provide regular field education training with opportunities for 'hands-on' experience in planning, conduct, and evaluation of liturgical celebrations within a congregational setting.

Liturgical training deals very much with the art of conduct and crafting of public worship. In our own seminary, we provide a wide fare of training programmes required for all students to ensure that they are 'at home' with every aspect of the liturgy. These programmes are separate from but not unrelated to the actual chapel services experienced by students. Using the seminary chapel as a 'laboratory', there is at least one training programme offered in each of the eight semesters of a student's general programme which includes: training for sacristanship, acolytate, lectorate, dynamics of liturgical chanting, choral singing, conducting and accompaniment, practice preaching, preaching in the parish setting (which is coordinated with the students' weekend field-work supervisors), and presiding at sacramental celebrations and conduct of special services.

A very common method of training liturgical leaders today involves the use of videotape in doing playbacks for group and self-criticism. After all, for most students, seeing is believing. The possibility of seeing how one led a service can be more convincing than simply being told not to frown or being instructed to look at people.[20] Every student ought to be able to see him/herself as the people will be seeing and hearing them for years to come. Then maybe they will realize what a privilege it is to lead God's people in worship.

Because the Book of Common Prayer provides a variety of options in terms of euchological formulae and ceremonial acts for various circumstances, another method commonly used in liturgical training is role-playing, where students are subjected to actual or imagined cases in parish life where decisions about worship have to be made. This gives them a chance to reflect on the theological and pastoral bases for decision-making.

It should be pointed out that liturgical training is not the same thing as teaching of rubrics, however important rubrics may be. Rubrics exist to guarantee that the liturgy be done well externally; but it is the content and spirit of the liturgy which must be given pride of place. One of the problems confronting seminary professors of liturgy is providing harmony between what is taught and how one actually leads in worship: 'Insensitive celebrants and inappropriate worship space and music take their toll. It is hard to teach the necessity of careful planning, preparation, and conduct of worship when students may be exposed daily to the opposite. Since so much gets taught by doing in the chapel that cannot be taught by precept in the classroom, it does seem important that there be continuity.'[21]

The New Instruction on Liturgical Formation in Seminaries from the Congregation for Catholic Education provides a general principle for us in this area:

Great care should be exercised in preparing the students to fulfill the office of moderator of the liturgy and president of the liturgical assembly by teaching them all things regarding a correct celebration of the liturgy, most especially holy Mass. However, there is a twofold distortion to be avoided in this: (1) the students should not consider and experience the liturgy as mere practice for learning their future roles. On the contrary, they must participate here and now in the liturgical mysteries taking due account of their present status. Their participation should be full, understanding and devout; (2) nor should those liturgical texts be chosen which, it might be presumed, are suitable to be used for the faithful in future pastoral work. Rather, it is better that they here and now experience all the riches of ecclesiastical prayer so that imbued with these, they might afterwards be able to communicate these riches to the faithful.[22]

Liturgical formation of ordinands

What ideally should the formation programme of any seminary seek to accomplish? In answer, it should be devoted primarily to the worship of God through the individual and collective actions of the seminarians and their faculty. It should try to sanctify the student both as an individual and as a social being. Insofar as s/he is an individual, it should try to secure from the seminarian the highest degree of response and commitment, and should provide ample opportunity for him/her to formulate this response and nurture this commitment. It should attempt to sanctify the entire day, rather than try to space the spiritual exercises for the purpose of leaving the rest of the day free for other activities. In the Anglican tradition, it should be structured around the Eucharist and the divine offices of Morning and Evening Prayer as the determining elements. It should develop a spiritual life for the priest who will serve the congregation rather than to make him/her live as a religious in that congregation.

The liturgy admirably serves as the binding force and integrating factor that unites and relates all the different acts of the spiritual programme into one coherent and meaningful whole.

Unfortunately, it is easy to confuse the integration of the spiritual programme with the liturgy with a large number of liturgical practices. The liturgical spirit does not proceed automatically from a multitude of ritual acts. Not uncommonly, scriptural devotions, cushions in place of missal stands, altars facing the assembly, the use of contemporary art, whole-wheat hosts, and a measured use of jargon can deceive both faculty and students into thinking that externals are the real worship of the church.

The seminary is a Christian microcosm. It is a small, rather complete, and largely isolated unit, which, in its own way, reflects the church at large. Within this microcosm, the students and faculty live both as individuals, each with his/her own problems and outlook, and as members of a community, a fact which adds dimension to their lives, brings them a new set of responsibilities, and provides the opportunity for even greater spiritual development by the fullest possible exercise of Christian charity and the formation of beneficial Christian relationships. In leading this communal life, the members have to relate and to adjust to a variety of levels. The liturgical-spiritual programme of the seminary strives to show the student how to sanctify his/her attitudes and relations toward others, and how to exercise them from a supernatural point of view. This s/he must do in union with all other aspects of his/her training; the spiritual life must, like all his/her other activities, be intrinsic to his/her ordinary activities. Eventually, s/he will have to formulate similar relations with those outside the seminary.

Thus it is that the seminary seeks to provide an atmosphere in which the student will be free to exercise as much as possible his/her baptismal character. Like the church at large, the individual student has been set aside – chosen – for the worship of God. As a Christian, this is his/her highest duty; as an ordained minister, this will be the raison d'être of his/her vocation, the one in which, as an instrument, s/he is actuated to produce an effect beyond the power of any created nature. If the seminary is truly to be a reflection of the church universal, it must be dedicated totally and completely to the worship of God. If this is done, then the spirit of that worship will infallibly permeate the other aspects of the seminary programme, without the need of any artificial or external integration.[23]

It is my conviction that the tone of life in a seminary is set by the Eucharist. Nothing is more important for life in the seminary itself and for the future life of ordinands than the experience of the Eucharist during their seminary days. It is of prime concern that the Eucharist is in reality a living, existential encounter with Christ on their part, and that this encounter is not limited to a five-minute Holy Communion span but rather that it is realized in all its external and social dimensions.

For the Eucharist to be this, every aspect of its celebration merits careful attention. It would seem that in this matter a total, existential approach is indicated. A total existential approach takes into account more than canonized formulae for the automatic production of the good priest. A total existential approach requires that we pay attention to the sharpening of the knowledge, skills and attitudes of today's candidates for ordination.

The Eucharist in the seminary must be adapted precisely to seminarians who are like no other group in the world; it must be celebrated *by* them rather than *for* them. This concept will mean a total re-evaluation of the celebration from every point of view. There is the matter of scheduling, for example. To celebrate the Eucharist in the morning, on the pretext that the day should begin with it, will have to be reconsidered to make sure that this is not just a means of getting it out of the way for the more important business at hand. The Eucharist should be celebrated when the seminarians can most fruitfully participate in it, whatever time of day this may be.

Naturally, manner of celebration is more important than time of celebration. But even granting the most propitious time and the best manner of celebration, the formative and educative role of the Eucharist will not be automatic. Seminary authorities will have to engage every device at their disposal, and will have to do this with a kind of infinite patience, to make the Eucharist the daily meaningful experience which it was instituted to be. The point is that the Eucharist must enter most intimately into the details of the daily life of the seminarian. If it remains aloof, separated from the seminarian's reach by some pious fiction of false respect, then s/he will not profit by it in the seminary and s/he will be even more surely unable to communicate its fruits later to his/her parishioners.[24]

Even more important than the external circumstances in which the Eucharist is offered, or the preparation for its offering, is the actual celebration of the banquet. To make the Eucharist a living and life-giving experience is certainly the work of the Spirit; however, the Spirit is active only where human-made conditions are welcoming. Cushioned kneelers, stained-glass windows, soft lights – these have virtually nothing to do with these human-made conditions. What is needed more than anything else is persons, persons especially in those who act as ministers, both the presiding celebrant and his/her co-offerers in the sacrifice. This concept of being a person, being a presider at the Eucharist in such a way that it is somewhat more than merely valid, is indefinable and even indescribable.

Thomas Krosnicki rightly insists that 'the relationship between liturgical praxis and ecclesial expression of faith and discipline is placed at the heart of the formation of candidates for the presbyterate. For if the church experiences the difficulty nowadays of reconciling the *lex credendi* and the *lex orandi* it is due in no small part to past liturgical formation in seminaries, and because seminaries today are still grappling with ways of finding a methodology to deal with the problem.'[25]

The issue of relating the seminary chapel services to actual parish celebration may be raised here. Planning worship for the seminary community with its particular needs can be a model of planning for those who, as parish pastors, will have to relate the tradition to the unique needs of a local congregation. Field experiences in parishes as a part of the basic seminary training should alert students to the differences between seminary and parish worship. But much would be gained if the liturgics professor was able to help students appreciate the fact that in the parishes they are not dealing with a situation which cannot digest the rich diet of the seminary chapel as much as with a completely different liturgical milieu.[26]

Is seminary the proper locus for liturgical education, training, and formation?

Is the seminary the proper setting for a wholistic/holistic preparation of future liturgical leaders? As Krosnicki pointed out, 'The relationship between seminary formation and its liturgical life and the liturgical-sacramental life of the parish which candidates are later to serve is crucial . . . For as long as liturgical celebrations within seminary walls remained perfunctory, or at best obsessed with a *Liber usualis* mentality, rather than what was variously described as a *liturgical spirit* or *liturgical sense*, future priests would carry over into their ministries that liturgical culture with which they were imbued in the seminary.'[27]

The seminary is a closed and artificial society, and in many ways it is monastic. It definitely does not correspond to the life of a parish. In the seminary, an ordinand is a member of the community; in the parish, s/he is the leader. In the seminary, s/he is a member of the liturgical assembly; in the parish, s/he is the celebrant. But most of all in the seminary, his/her liturgical practices are performed in common with others. In the parish, this group environment may be lacking. The parish may also lack many of the liturgical practices to which s/he has grown accustomed, and it may fall far behind the church universal in developing a liturgical life.

It is to be noted too, that the academic calendar followed by most seminaries does not give the students an experience of the full sweep of the liturgical year. The lack caused by this has to be deliberately complemented by the field education programme of the seminary, preferably one that is parish-based, where students can experience the celebration of some of the important feast days and days of fasting within the framework of the liturgical seasons.

It should be emphasized that the liturgical-spiritual programme of the seminary, as opposed to liturgical courses, is intended to sanctify the student and mature him/her spiritually by offering the ideal means of worshipping God in common with other members of the mystical Body. It is not a course in pastoral liturgy whose purpose is to accustom the student to certain liturgical practices so that s/he can later introduce them into priestly work. The liturgy must perfect a person, this particular individual, this member of the Christian community. This person must have an opportunity to make both a personal and a social response to God. If this training has its proper effect, then the priest will have a high regard for his/her own worth as an individual, will find and appreciate this same worth in the people s/he serves, and will appreciate his/her own position in the church and the responsibilities it entails. His/her own personal development and degree of liturgical perfection and understanding will be of greatest help in approaching parochial ministry and in building a spiritual life which is an integral part of it.[28]

Final word

When a person is ordained, s/he becomes a liturgist in the full and proper sense of the term. His/her own life must be formed around the principles of the liturgy. S/he must communicate the life of the church to others, both as celebrant of the Christian mysteries and as dispenser of the word of God – through him/her the faithful are brought into contact with both the incarnate and the inspired Word.

Daniel B. Stevick rightly pointed out that 'Good liturgy does not come about by accident. Even a simple liturgical event has some complexity. Many things happen in a brief time . . . Elements can compete with or subvert one another . . . Runaway virtuosity can heighten some nonessential action, while important acts are allowed to pass unnoticed. Or the liturgical event can be experienced as a series of parts that follow one another without shape, consecutiveness or flow.'[29]

As suggested by the title of Stevick's book, shaping good liturgy is a craft. Rather than being a science, it is an art, calling for taste, judgement, and design. It requires a practical sense of the possibilities and limitations of one's spatial and musical resources. Like good and spontaneous-seeming dance or drama, it may require timing and practice. And those who make the advance preparations for a liturgical act must learn to be self-critical. Not every idea that comes to mind – not even every good idea – can be used. The blue pencil is a valuable tool of those who prepare liturgy. Good intentions are not enough.[30]

As priests, we take seriously our responsibility to preside at the liturgy with care and humility: with care that all is in order, with humility in recognizing that it is not we who make God's presence real, but that it is our role to allow that presence to be made manifest and not to obstruct God's working. Simplicity bids and binds us to keep 'out of the way'. Work towards cohesive celebration is implied in liturgy, for it is in liturgy that creation comes face to face with the mystery that is God.[31]

I fully agree with my colleague Louis Weil, who opines that many of the liturgical woes experienced by congregations due to ineffective presidency by clergy can be attributed to simply 'lack of common sense'. Common sense operates fully well only when presidency is approached with confidence that can only come from years of experience in participating in the liturgy combined with proper education, training, and formation.

Notes

1 Daniel B. Stevick, *The Crafting of Liturgy* (New York: Church Hymnal Corporation, 1990), p. 33.

2 'The ordered, somewhat complex actions of worship usually require a presiding person, even if such a central person acts in collaboration with other ministers. And the persons who are called and set apart to fill this central role in and for the liturgical assembly must come to terms with the special prerogatives and restraints it carries. Liturgical presidency in the Christian community is marked by a fundamental modesty. It is not a performance in which one's gifts or one's personality are put on display. Affectation and self-importance are out of place. It is a

representative, pastoral role whose bonds with a people are created and sustained by love and care. Presidential leadership is made effective by a strange reciprocity; if the worship of the people depends on trusted leaders, the effectiveness of liturgical leaders depends, to a great extent, on the trust that is extended to them.' Ibid., p. 32.

3 Stevick declares, 'In some liturgical functions, leadership may be taken by any competent person; but the Church reserves presidency in its central sacramental rites to those who are set apart as bishops and priests. (Whether these central roles are always, and necessarily, to be so reserved is under some discussion today, and the issues are not simple.) Anglicans would contend theologically that the ordained ministries are, in some sense, God-given . . . Even though the ministry is God-given, it was originally, and continues to be, given through social and historical means.' Ibid., pp. 32–3.

4 Dennis G. Michno, *A Priest's Handbook: The Ceremonies of the Church* (2nd edn, Wilton, CT: Morehouse-Barlow, 1986), p. 13.

5 Nathan Mitchell, 'Liturgical Education in Roman Catholic Seminaries: A Report and an Appraisal', *Worship* 54 (1980): 129.

6 The *Constitution on the Sacred Liturgy* (Article 16) commends that 'in theological faculties, the study of the liturgy must be ranked among the principal courses. It is to be taught under its theological, historical, spiritual, pastoral and juridical aspects'. *Vatican Council II: The Conciliar and Post Conciliar Documents*, ed. Austin Flannery, OP (new revised edn, Northport, NY: Costello Publishing Company, 1984); henceforth all texts cited from this document will be designated 'SC' (*Sacrosanctum concilium*) followed by the article number.

7 I am borrowing here an expression from the *Constitution on the Sacred Liturgy*.

8 Maur Burbach OSB, 'Liturgical Education in the Seminary', in *Seminary Education in a Time of Change*, eds James Michael Lee and Louis J. Putz (Notre Dame, IN: Fides Publishers, 1965), p. 431.

9 'Thus when, week by week, and year by year, the person of our Lord and His deeds were presented to the minds of the faithful, they could realize what it means to be a Christian. So long as the faithful understood this language and were moved by it, they could not go astray, even if their knowledge of the contents of the faith was otherwise slight, or if they were unacquainted with the finer distinctions being made by theologians. And we can understand how, through centuries, a ministry of souls was possible that knew nothing of any systematic catechesis, in which there was little preaching and that usually by the bishop only, and in which instruction by means of printed words was not yet possible. Nevertheless Christianity flourished and was vitally alive – because the

great truths of Christianity were learned and were a living experience in the liturgy.' Josef Jungmann, SJ, *The Assisi Papers* (Collegeville, MN: Liturgical Press, 1957), p. 25.

10 *Acta Apostolica Sedis* XVII (December 1925), p. 603; translated and cited by Maur Burbach, 'Liturgical Education in the Seminary', p. 432.

11 Mark Searle offers an incisive treatment of the 'Pedagogical Function of the Liturgy' in *Worship* 55 (1981): 332–59.

12 James White observed that while modern liturgical scholarship began more than a century and a half ago, the teaching of liturgy as a major subject in North American seminaries is a phenomenon largely dating from the 1960s. 'Some Lessons in Liturgical Pedagogy', *Worship* 68 (1994): 438.

13 In Roman Catholic seminaries, the impetus was provided by SC 16: 'The study of sacred liturgy is to be ranked among the compulsory and major courses in seminaries and religious houses of studies. In theological faculties is it to rank among the principal courses. It is to be taught under its theological, historical, spiritual, pastoral, and juridical aspects . . .'

14 Mark Searle observes that 'Ever since liturgiology became something more than the study of rubrics, the study of the liturgy has been regarded as a predominantly historical discipline.' 'New Tasks, New Methods: The Emergence of Pastoral Liturgical Studies', *Worship* 57 (1984): 291.

15 Mark Searle himself argues that 'the study of liturgy in the life of the church today is too important to be entrusted to anyone else but liturgists', ibid., p. 294.

16 James F. White, 'The Teaching of Worship in Seminaries in Canada and the United States', *Worship* 55 (1981): 316.

17 White, 'Some Lessons in Liturgical Pedagogy', *Worship* 68 (1994): 440.

18 Nathan Mitchell, 'Liturgical Education in Roman Catholic Seminaries', *Worship* 54 (1980): 137. In a survey he conducted among major Roman Catholic seminaries in the U.S., Mitchell singled out a Midwestern seminary where the course on 'fundamental theology' followed an interdisciplinary format which includes lecture, seminar, and discussion periods with involvement by professors drawn from all the major departments: biblical studies; systematics; moral/ethics; pastoral; liturgy/communications. He also acknowledged that satisfactory curricular integration is only one aspect of a much larger problem: the contribution of all the major theological disciplines to the student's personal and professional preparation for the ordained ministry, a most fundamental problem facing seminary faculties today.

19 White, 'The Teaching of Worship in Seminaries in Canada and the United States', *Worship* 55 (1981): 318.

20 Ibid., p. 312.

21 Ibid., pp. 313–14.

22 Sacred Congregation for Catholic Education, *Instruction on Liturgical Formation in Seminaries* (Rome: Typis Polyglottis Vaticanis, 1979); cited from http://www.ewtn.com/library/curia/ccesems.htm; accessed 23/07/2009.

23 Stafford Poole, *Seminary in Crisis* (New York: Herder and Herder, 1965), pp. 132–3.

24 Burbach, 'Liturgical Education in the Seminary', p. 431.

25 Thomas Krosnicki, 'Seminary Liturgy Revisited', *Worship* 54 (1980): 159.

26 Frank C. Senn, 'Teaching Worship in Seminaries: A Response', *Worship* 55 (1981): 330.

27 Krosnicki, 'Seminary Liturgy Revisited', p. 160.

28 Poole, *Seminary in Crisis*, pp. 134–5.

29 Stevick, *The Crafting of Liturgy*, p. 5.

30 Ibid., p. 6.

31 Michno, *A Priest's Handbook*, p. 18.

6

'WHEN WILL YOU MAKE AN END?'

An Agenda for Continuing Liturgical Education

Richard Geoffrey Leggett

Introduction

When I was twelve, my parents took my sister and me to see the film *The Agony and the Ecstasy*, starring Charlton Heston as Michelangelo and Rex Harrison as Pope Julius II. The film's core narrative focuses on Michelangelo's painting of the Sistine Chapel and his stormy relationship with the Pope. At one point in the film, Julius, frustrated by many starts and delays, shouts at Michelangelo, who is perched on the scaffolding, 'When will you make an end?' 'When I am finished,' responds Michelangelo.

Some years ago at a gathering of the Anglican members of the North American Academy of Liturgy, Professor Paul Bradshaw remarked that the work of liturgical renewal was far from complete. Although numerous revisions of liturgical texts had been undertaken and, in some cases, brought to conclusion for the time being, the work of liturgical *formation* was just beginning. After all, Jesus warned us that new wine required new skins, and new texts require new perspectives on the part of those who use them.

Since Professor Bradshaw made these remarks, the situation has not significantly changed. New liturgical texts have appeared in various provinces of the Anglican Communion as well as challenges to the very premise that Anglican worship requires the use of common liturgical texts. If I reflect on my own experience as a presbyter of the Anglican Church of Canada, I can identify a growing diversity of worship practices within my own province: (i) strict adherence to the Prayer Book of 1962, (ii) flexible adherence to the Prayer Book, (iii) strict adherence to *The Book of Alternative Services* (1985), (iv) flexible adherence to *The Book of Alternative Services*, (v) use of both resources and/or supplemental resources prepared by diocesan and national authorities, (vi) use of worship resources from other Anglican provinces, and (vii) use of worship resources and styles from non-Anglican sources.

My own diocesan bishop, in response to a diocesan strategic planning process that identified a broadly based desire to re-imagine and renew Anglican worship, re-formed a diocesan advisory commission on liturgy that includes the following in its mandate:

- to work with the diocesan bishop on opportunities for education and reflection on the role of liturgy in the life of the church;
- to seek to offer liturgical expression in a manner that reflects Anglican history and experience in a culture of West Coast spirituality;
- to hold workshops annually for diocesan clergy and lay leaders on liturgical principles and the changing shape of liturgy, bringing to the diocese people with expertise in the study and practice of liturgy.

As a member of the faculty of Vancouver School of Theology for more than twenty years, it has become abundantly clear to me that the liturgical reforms of the past forty years have not yet permeated into all the congregations of the Anglican Church of Canada. I suspect that many of us, if not all, could make the same observation about our own diocesan and national churches.

We continue to pursue the revision and development of texts without, in my opinion, an on-going commitment to liturgical formation and education. New texts without a clear understanding of liturgical principles will not renew the worship life of the Christian communities to which we belong.

Living as I do in a province whose economy and world-view are shaped in part by vast forests, some of great antiquity, I realize that many clergy and educated laity cannot distinguish between forests and trees. They have not learned that the forest in which we worship is formed by a variety of different but interrelated flora and fauna. A forest requires the interaction of a number of things in order for it to be a genuine forest. Unfortunately, too many of our clergy and laity are busily importing or removing trees without understanding how those trees function within the living forest of worship. They create the theological and pastoral equivalent of tree farms rather than the more complex ecosystem we know as a forest.

Since I became a member of the faculty in 1987, I have travelled throughout Canada and the United States as well as teaching expeditions to the Solomon Islands and Burma (Myanmar). These forays bring me much joy, and I learn a great deal from them. But they also cause me some concern. I am learning that some of our clergy are leaving their theological colleges and other training programmes with an insufficient grounding in liturgical studies, that is to say, an understanding of how liturgy works, how symbol works, and how liturgy gives expression to our theology, our understanding of who God is and what God does and is doing and, we hope, will do. As important as it is for ordained and lay leaders of worship to know their way around the official liturgical resources of their churches, it is also important that they understand the historical, theological, and pastoral dimensions of the liturgical rites that find expression in these resources. The decline in the formal liturgical education of both clergy and laity means that continuing education carries an increasing burden of responsibility.

In preparation for the original presentation of this paper in August 2003 for the Cuddeson session of the International

Anglican Liturgical Consultation, I wrote to the bishops of the Anglican Church of Canada to solicit their perspectives on the following question: 'If I were designing a programme of continuing education in liturgy for the clergy of the diocese, I would . . . ' Half of the bishops responded, some with wide-ranging answers, others focusing on a shorter list of needs. What I gained from the exercise was a greater appreciation of the insights of Thomas Long.

Thomas G. Long is the Bandy Professor of Preaching at Candler School of Theology in Atlanta, Georgia. He received a grant from the Lilly Endowment in the United States to conduct research in an effort to move beyond the debate between the supporters of the so-called 'seeker' worship and the supporters of what might be described as the ecumenical consensus reflected in *Baptism, Eucharist and Ministry* and the work of the post-Vatican II liturgical movement. His research resulted in a small book, published by the Alban Institute in the United States, entitled *Beyond the Worship Wars: Building Vital and Faithful Worship*.[1] In this book Professor Long identifies nine characteristics of vital and faithful worship.

These characteristics confirm my own experience and those of the bishops who responded to my inquiry. I shall return to Professor Long's work later in this chapter. But before I do so, I want to comment on the title to this chapter.

'When will you make an end?' While I believe that what I write has application in more than one liturgical setting, there is no doubt in my mind that there can be no single agenda for the continuing education of clergy and laity in the area of liturgy, nor that we can ever declare the task complete. Each province, perhaps each diocese, faces the challenge of responding to its own context. I have given an example from my own diocese, where my bishop seeks to address the missional needs of a minority church in a culture where most consider the church or any religious community irrelevant at best, pernicious at worst. In other contexts the questions will be different, but we cannot act as if the task is not a pressing one, nor a task that will one day disappear from our agenda as people of faith.

Those of us for whom the ritual life of the gathered Christian assembly continues to be life-giving and life-shaping are Michelangelo to our culture's Julius. Despite repeated calls to make an end, we are not finished. In this spirit I venture to make five suggestions for continuing education in the area of liturgy and worship.

Suggestion 1: The continuing education of clergy and laity in the area of liturgy and worship needs to encourage liturgical leadership to make room for the experience of mystery.[2]

One of the approaches that I have found helpful in working with a group of laity or clergy is to ask them two questions: 'What has been your most significant experience of worship?' and 'Why was this experience so significant for you?' These two questions lead us into some reflection, as a group, on why these experiences were so significant and into an exploration of the meaning of 'mystery' in our religious lives.

In his response to my inquiry regarding continuing education, Archbishop David Crawley, sometime Bishop of Kootenay and Archbishop of British Columbia and Yukon, wrote that

> Generation Xers are, in practical terms . . . 'post modern'. For them, in matters of faith, verification is experiential and the experiences that they need to find in the church are worship that provides a sense of the Holy and a community they feel will be there for them. I would therefore frame a programme of continuing education around the first of those needs, worship with a sense of the holy.

He continued, 'I would focus on how to create a Holy space, looking at what elements evoke a sense of holiness, examining how decoration, movement, use, discipline and preparation contribute to it.'[3]

Archbishop Crawley's remarks are echoed by Professor Long in his study of the worship life of congregations:

> [W]e need to join ourselves in community with others to give ourselves away to God, to offer our lives to something larger

than ourselves, something that provides meaning and lets us know that our lives count for something of ultimate value.[4]

Additionally, Long notes that vital and faithful worship is characterized (a) by creative adaptation of the space and environment for worship and (b) by forging a strong connection between worship and local mission.[5]

This means several things. First, clergy and laity need to learn how the space and environment for worship shape the actual worship experiences of believers. The *domus ecclesiae Dei* is formed by many spaces, such as gathering space, congregational space, movement space, baptismal space, choir space, and altar space. When the use of these spaces remains static, they cease to release their potential to be revelations of the *mystērion* of God being enacted in the liturgical assembly. Consequently, clergy and laity need to be encouraged to consider, even in churches with inflexible seating arrangements and fixed furniture, how these spaces can be released to surprise us with new insights into our life as Christ's Body.

Second, clergy and laity need to understand the power of symbol. Too often have I heard a presbyter or a deacon or a bishop or a lay leader mutter, 'It's *only* symbolic.' When I hear those words, I know that I may be in the presence of someone who is losing or has lost a sense of wonder, an openness to surprise, and an ability to let objects and actions speak. Aidan Kavanagh writes that

> One who is convinced that symbol and reality are mutually exclusive should avoid the liturgy. Such a one should also avoid poetry, concerts and the theatre, language, loving another person, and most other attempts at communicating with one's kind. Symbol is reality at its most intense degree of being expressed. One resorts to symbol when reality swamps all other forms of discourse. This happens regularly when one approaches God with others, as in the liturgy. Symbol is thus as native to liturgy as metaphor is to language. One learns to live with symbol and metaphor or gives up the ability to speak or to worship communally.[6]

When vestments are left to fray, books to decay, banners to unravel, then their ability to communicate is diminished. When readers read from flimsy pieces of paper rather than from books of sufficient dignity to carry the weight of the Word, when the silence between the words 'Let us pray' and the opening line of a collect collapses into a nanosecond, then their ability to communicate is diminished. When baptismal water is reduced to an imperceptible sprinkle and eucharistic bread to an object unrecognizable as a source of life, then symbolic meaning is at risk.

Artists, poets, dancers, and actors can lend us their skills and knowledge to help us understand the power of the drama to connect us with the unfolding *mystērion* we call salvation history. We can renew our ability to use vision, language, movement, and voice to convey a sense of the holy.[7]

Third, it is not enough to attend to liturgical aesthetics and performance alone. We need to help our clergy and laity articulate their understanding of the *missio Dei*, their understanding of what God is doing in the world and how Christians, corporately and personally, participate in that *missio*.[8] Liturgy is a corporate act of public service voluntarily performed for the common good of the whole creation by those who have been called by God to this work. In other words, liturgy that does not transform and empower us for public witness, for justice, and for the self-giving service of others is theological narcissism.

Spending a day on baptism and confirmation without time spent on asking ourselves the question 'How does baptism or confirmation serve the *missio Dei*?' is a day half-spent. Learning how to make liturgical space more communicative without identifying the message we are attempting to communicate is moving deck chairs on a sinking ship.

Liturgy that talks about justice but does not do justice is not liturgy. If we are not careful about the roles, the persons, the texts, and the actions we use in worship, then we are not involved in proclaiming a mystery, we are simply being mysterious. Language matters. Gestures matter. When the same people have been the ministers of communion for the last twenty-five years with no alteration, the mystery of every baptized person as an embodiment of the life-giving Christ is a bit lost.

Finally, if we are truly to shape an appreciation of the mystery at work in the liturgy, then clergy and laity need to be able to shape a community of prayer, a community in which both communal and personal prayer is offered and modelled, modelled not on monastic models but on secular models, secular in the best meaning of the word, 'in the world', engaged in the reality we face day to day.

Suggestion 2: The continuing education of clergy and laity in liturgy and worship needs to enable them to make planned and concerted efforts to show hospitality to the stranger.[9]

For more than twenty years I have been involved in the theological formation of aboriginal and non-aboriginal people who are engaged in pastoral ministry in aboriginal communities in Canada and the United States. One of the key aspects of my work is helping students identify the *trans-cultural*, *counter-cultural*, *cross-cultural* and *contextual* dimensions of Christian worship that either help or hinder the ritual communication of the good news of God in Jesus Christ.[10]

This work has convinced me that the dominant or majority culture tends to consider inculturation as a dimension of ministry to other ethnic or racial communities rather than a dynamic process that is at work within the dominant or majority culture itself. If clergy and laity are to offer effective leadership in the area of liturgy and worship, then they will need to understand the process of inculturation and the four dimensions identified above. This leads me to a series of brief questions that might shape a programme of continuing education in inculturation.

- *Trans-cultural*: How do we determine those aspects of Christian faith and practice that transcend cultural identities and unite Christians in all times and places? How do we deal with the differences that exist between Christians when we disagree on those aspects?
- *Counter-cultural*: How do we identify those aspects of our culture which are life-denying rather than life-giving? How does Christian faith and practice form us for resistance?

- *Contextual*: Who are the people in the pews? Who are the people who are not in the pews? Why are they not in the pews? How does our exercise of Christian faith and practice include the 'other', however we define 'other'? How does it exclude the 'other'?
- *Cross-cultural*: How can we experience other cultural expressions of Christian faith and practice on the terms of the 'other' rather than as theological voyeurs? How do we distinguish between a Christian fad and a Christian culture?

Another aspect of making room for the stranger is the conduct of the pastoral offices of the church. Weddings, reconciliation of a penitent, ministry with the sick, and funerals continue to be opportunities when the 'un-churched' or the 'alienated' cross cautiously over the invisible boundary marking the dispersed church from the gathered assembly. How we conduct such occasions may determine the future course of a seeker after Christ.

Finally, clergy and laity need to consider how the Word is proclaimed in the liturgical assembly. Time after time the bishops and others whom I have encountered have expressed their concern.

> Liturgy is public worship on behalf of the whole community. The Word speaks not only to the Church but to the world and the struggles it engages.[11]
>
> . . . ensure courses in effective preaching and the public reading of Holy Scripture.[12]
>
> . . . I would re-emphasize the sermon, not how to preach, that is the subject for another kind of continuing education, but the place of the sermon in the liturgy.[13]
>
> . . . encourage an understanding of the lectionary . . . [14]

Understanding the structure and dynamic of the lectionaries in use in our churches, reading the scriptures clearly and for meaning as well emphasizing the sermon as a proclamation of the Word, its release into our midst to work its continuing transformation and transfiguration of those who hear it, all these are continuing challenges for the clergy and laity of our churches.

Suggestion 3: The continuing education of clergy and laity in liturgy and worship needs to enable them to recover and make visible the sense of drama inherent in Christian worship.[15]

For many clergy and laity the liturgy, as I have commented above, is a collection of trees rather than a dynamic sylvan eco-system. They are unaware of the basic structure of the western liturgy: gathering, proclamation, prayer, sacramental focus, and commissioning.[16] This lack of understanding compromises their ability to plan liturgical celebrations that are dramatic in the best sense of the word, celebrations that help us encounter and ex-plore truth. Consequently gathering and commissioning rites take dimensions far beyond their role in bringing the assembly to-gether and sending it forth in mission. Proclamation is reduced to the reading of biblical texts and the recitation of a psalm or canticle rather than the release into our midst of the living Word with all its power. Genuine prayer is often replaced by the me-chanical recitation of prepared texts rather than the more risky business of composing intercessions based on the needs and con-cerns of the people gathered for the occasion.

In the Anglican tradition these five structural units of our litur-gical rites are put into motion by specific liturgical 'muscles' such as the greeting and collect of the gathering rite, the scriptural texts and reflections of the proclamation, to name but a few. Most of the other familiar elements serve to elucidate the occa-sion or season rather than serve as fixed elements of every cel-ebration. Clergy and laity require continued education to learn how to distinguish between what is necessary in a liturgical rite, i.e., the primary structures and muscles, and what elaborates and enhances the given occasion or season. The people of God have the right to experience Advent as Advent and Lent as Lent rather than ordinary time in blue or purple.

This leads me to observe that many clergy and laity still do not understand the dynamic of the liturgical year. Rather than look at the two cycles that celebrate the incarnation and the resurrec-tion, many clergy and laity look at Sundays as separate pearls on a string. In doing so they lose sight of the movement of the Spirit throughout a given cycle that brings us to its ritual climax in the celebration of the baptism of Christ or the sending of the Holy Spirit.

Ordinary time has its own dynamic as well. Recent liturgical reform is not limited to the distribution of texts to cover the Sundays after Epiphany until Ash Wednesday and those after Trinity to the First Sunday of Advent. The Revised Common Lectionary and other lectionaries provide either thematic or narrative schemes that can be used to engage the worshipper in the mystery of a God who is active in time.[17] For those who use the Revised Common Lectionary, for example, the David cycle in Year B begs for some homiletical treatment as we move through the betrayal of Uriah to the prophetic judgement of Nathan. How shall we understand a God who is willing to enter into an eternal covenant with a man who is guilty of adultery and murder?

But good drama involves more than just a good story. It is also the actions of individual actors in company with others who act out their roles. Liturgical continuing education must assist clergy and laity to be more attentive to the *quality* of the celebration.[18] How we use our voices, the gestures we make to accentuate prayer texts, and the arrangement and decoration of space all combine to help us enact the drama of salvation.

Recent reforms in our understanding of ministry and of the role of the community in the liturgical assembly require us to consider how the presider serves as the conductor of the assembly's symphony, as Aidan Kavanagh explains:

11. *The liturgical assembly is less a gathering of individuals than a dynamic co-ordination of orders.*
These orders are catechumens, servers, penitents, deacons, the baptized faithful, presbyters, and bishops. Each of these groups, in transacting their own business both in and out of the liturgy, contributes to the consummation of the business of the whole assembly both in and out of the liturgy . . . Thus their shared witness, charisms, obligations, and styles all contribute in rich diversity to the Church's ministry of reconciliation. It is a central part of the pastoral art to be able to discern, respect,

and co-ordinate the rich gifts of these orders both in and out of the liturgy for the good of the Church and the world to which the Church is corporate minister by God's grace.[19]

In too many congregations the actual celebration of the liturgy and its planning are conducted by the presider who may simply need some encouragement and additional knowledge to move into a more corporate and authentic spirit of liturgical celebration.

> The liturgical minister is not the poet but only the reciter of the poet's poem – the poet in this case being the Christian assembly past and present.[20]

Suggestion 4: The continuing education of clergy and laity in liturgy and worship will emphasize congregational music that is both excellent and eclectic in style and genre.[21]

The professor who taught parish administration in my theological college used case studies to help us work through the various issues associated with parish life and the role of the rector as the chief operating officer. The very first case study we used was entitled 'How to fire the organist'. Long uses a different image but one which describes the situation that many parish clergy and laity find themselves in today as regards the musical life of their congregations:

> Music is the nuclear reactor of congregational worship. It is where much of the radioactive material is stored, where a good bit of the energy is generated, and, alas, where congregational meltdown is most likely to occur. Change the order of worship, and you may set off a debate. Change the style of music, and you may split the congregation.[22]

Despite these risks clergy and laity must be able to offer leadership in a time when music can become what one of my colleagues called the 'war department' of the congregation.

Clergy and laity need to learn how to identify music that is *congregational*, *excellent*, and *eclectic*. By *congregational* I mean music that focuses on what the gathered community is gathered to do. Music sung by the choir can be congregational if it serves the liturgical action rather than the egos of the performers. Instrumental music can be congregational if it enables the congregation to reflect on the work of God in them and in the world rather than an interlude to deflect our attention while the liturgical minister does something else. To make such decisions clergy and laity need to have a clear sense of what are the movements within the liturgical action and how music, whether vocal or instrumental, whether congregational or choral, serves the liturgical action rather than the liturgical action serving the music.

By *excellent* I mean music that has both roots and wings, that both comforts and challenges, that is both familiar and strange. Excellent music uses texts that may strengthen us in times of uncertainty and difficulty, but there will also be texts which disturb us and shake us from the lethargy that can grip us from time to time. Clergy and laity need to learn how to be critical of texts and musical styles which dull us with banality. Such decisions can only be made when the clergy can articulate a clear, personal understanding of the gospel and its implications for Christian faith and practice.

Finally, by *eclectic* I mean this: No one style or genre of music has an exclusive claim on Christian loyalty. Depending upon the moment in the liturgical action, the particular liturgical occasion, or the season, a simple repetitive chant can bear as much gospel freight as a Reformation chorale or the latest composition of an English cathedral musician. Clergy and laity need to learn how to determine when a particular style or genre furthers the liturgical action and formation rather than being based solely upon the personal taste of the liturgical leadership.

Suggestion 5: The continuing education of clergy and laity in liturgy and worship will form clergy who are strong, loving and wise.[23]

In his influential reflection on liturgical presidency, Robert Hovda (of blessed memory) describes the qualifications of the presider.

Appropriate qualifications for the ordained clergy (particular places and times may add others) are: 1) depth and commitment of faith; 2) native talent, especially the particular and crucial talent of openness to others, respect for the charisms of others, and willingness to share responsibility with others as 'one who cares'; 3) desire and feeling of call; 4) adequate training for the function in question; 5) accomplishment or proved aptitude in apprenticeship; 6) a call and mandate from a church, a faith community; and, finally, 7) a commitment to continuing education.[24]

I would like to build upon these qualifications by reflecting on how continuing education can help clergy and laity be strong, loving, and wise.

Being 'strong' means knowing the whole story: One way in which liturgical presiders can become strong is by knowing the tradition thoroughly. Not only their own tradition but the broader catholic and ecumenical tradition can become sources of strength by freeing the presider from the prison of uncompromising particularity. The catholic and ecumenical tradition teaches us to be wary of the comment 'We've *never* done it that way', as well as its fraternal twin 'We've *always* done it that way'. There may be reasons why we have or have not chosen a particular course of action, but we need to be aware that it was a choice based on reasons that may or may not be applicable to our present context.

Being 'loving' means knowing how to lead the pilgrim people: Each one of us has a vision of what he or she believes the church can be, and the church's liturgy can become the ritual expression of that ideal. But we are daily confronted with the church as it is. If ordained and lay leadership has hopes of leading a congregation from one expression of worship into another, then they will need to know how to do this in a way which builds up the community rather than becomes the exercise of ministerial prerogative. Genuine change, genuine transformation, requires trust, trust between ordained and lay leadership and the community.

Being 'wise' means engaging in theological discourse rather than religious slogans: In a world fascinated with technique rather than meaning, with data rather than knowledge, with slogans rather than genuine discourse, Christian congregations need to become houses of wisdom. Wisdom comes from exposure to as many theological voices as possible and requires the willingness to go beneath the surface of our day-to-day lives to discover what God may be up to in them. Discussions about trinitarian language, about language that is faithful and fair to all God's people, and about who may participate in which sacraments and why they may or may not are not academic questions. Clergy and laity need opportunities to engage in discussions rather than debates so that they can enable similar discussions among the people they serve.

Conclusion

I close with a few comments about method. My own experience and the reflections of the bishops of my church suggest that the continuing education of the clergy and laity in the area of liturgy and worship cannot be done in isolation. Whenever possible, continuing education in liturgy and worship must bring together all those who exercise leadership in the church's liturgical assemblies, whether these persons are lay or ordained. Further, such education is enhanced when it provides ample opportunity for the interaction of the participants with each other. Finally, topics are not always as important as finding presenters who can impart their passion and vision in such a way as to renew and empower our liturgical leaders.

Probably, in the end, the educational events would be chosen by the options available to find life-giving presenters, rather than by the particular piece of liturgy to be addressed. So, you see, I do not have a need for particularly erudite and fascinating insights, so much as need to continue to fan into flame the spirits of those who worship, beginning with the clergy.[25]

This means that we have to develop diocesan, regional, and national strategies. There is, to my knowledge, no strategy for continuing education in the Anglican Church of Canada even though the General Synod reserves a claim to exercise some authority in the area of theological education. We have a national continuing education scheme that provides funding. We are, therefore, dependent upon the personal initiative and perceived needs of individual clergy and, in some cases, diocesan continuing education programmes. There is a tendency in institutions such as ours to be reactive rather than proactive.

For example, we introduced a major new hymn book in the late 1990s with a meagre budget for its presentation to the people of our church. Once the book was published, we did not follow up with a strategy for the continuing education of clergy and lay professionals in liturgical music. This is an unfortunate circumstance given the decline in the number of musicians trained for liturgical leadership, the conflicts around musical styles, and the importance of music as a dimension of corporate worship.

In contrast, our sisters and brothers in the Evangelical Lutheran Church in Canada had the benefit of funding to provide many events when *Evangelical Lutheran Worship* was introduced. The commitment to continuing education regarding liturgy and worship among the Lutheran community is further evident in the biennial National Worship Conference. One of the benefits of our full communion agreement (2001) for Canadian Anglicans is the gradual transformation of the National Worship Conference into a joint project of our two churches.

The General Synod of 2007 asked the Faith, Worship and Ministry Committee to present an agenda and principles for the revision of our contemporary liturgical texts to the General Synod of 2010. As I write this chapter, the first draft of this document has been prepared and is being reviewed prior to its being shared with the wider church. If the Anglican Church of Canada were to embark on the process leading to a revision of *The Book of Alternative Services* or some other resource or set of resources, would we ensure that there was a process of ongoing education to introduce these new resources to our people? Would we commit ourselves to a lengthy post-production familiarization with the theological and pastoral implications of the new rites? The present financial climate does not create an abundance of confidence that the answer to either question would be an unqualified 'yes'.

Some years ago, William Seth Adams, my predecessor once-removed at Vancouver School of Theology and retired professor of liturgical studies at the Seminary of the Southwest in Austin, Texas, suggested that we might consider establishing a College of Liturgists modelled after the College of Preachers in Washington, DC. Since preaching normally takes place within the liturgical assembly, perhaps it would be good to continue to hone the liturgical as well as homiletical skills of our clergy and laity. The vision, however, awaits its time.

'When will you make an end?' 'When I am finished.' I end where I began. More than four decades of liturgical revision have passed, but the work of liturgical formation continues. The suggestions for the continuing education in liturgy and worship for clergy and laity that I have set before you are not beyond our reach even if they will never pass away. So long as we proclaim a living God, we will need to form our hearts and minds for liturgical assemblies that also live and, living, must adapt and evolve to ensure an authentic engagement with this God.

When will we make an end? When we are finished. When will we be finished? Only when Christ comes to establish in its fullness the reign of God. Until then, our work continues.

Notes

1 Thomas G. Long, *Beyond the Worship Wars: Building Vital and Faithful Worship* (Washington, DC: The Alban Institute, 2001).

2 Ibid., p. 13.

3 Personal letter from David Crawley to Richard Leggett, 27 May 2003.

4 Long, p. 19.

5 Ibid., p. 13.

6 Aidan Kavanagh, *Elements of Rite: A Handbook of Liturgical Style* (New York, NY: Pueblo, 1982), p. 103.

7 See Kathleen Harmon, *The Mystery We Celebrate, the Song We Sing: A Theology of Liturgical Music* (Collegeville, MN: Liturgical Press, 2008) regarding the importance of the human voice in worship.

8 See J. G. Davies, *Worship and Mission* (New York, NY: Association Press, 1967); Gordon W. Lathrop, 'Liturgy and Mission in the North American Context', and Thomas H. Schattauer, 'Liturgical Assembly as Locus of Mission', *Inside Out: Worship in an Age of Mission*, ed. Thomas H. Schattauer (Minneapolis, MN: Fortress Press, 1999), pp. 201–12 and 1–21.

9 Long, p. 13.

10 For a further discussion of these terms see The Evangelical Lutheran Church in America, *Principles for Worship*, Renewing Worship 2 (Minneapolis, MN: Augsburg Fortress, 2002), pp. ix–x.

11 Electronic correspondence from Archbishop Andrew Hutchison to Richard Leggett, 4 March 2003.

12 Personal letter from then Bishop Terry Buckle (later Archbishop of British Columbia and Yukon) to Richard Leggett, 11 March 2003.

13 Crawley to Leggett.

14 Buckle to Leggett.

15 Long, p. 13.

16 See Paul Gibson, *Patterns of Celebration: Layers of Meaning in the Structure of the Eucharist* (Toronto, ON: Anglican Book Centre, 1998).

17 Consultation on Common Texts, *The Revised Common Lectionary* (Winfield, BC: Wood Lake Books, 1992); Consultation on Common Texts, *Revised Common Lectionary Daily Readings* (Minneapolis, MN: Fortress Press, 2005); Consultation on Common Texts, *Revised Common Lectionary Prayers Proposed by the Consultation on Common Texts* (Minneapolis, MN: Fortress Press, 2002).

18 See James F. White, *Sacraments as God's Self Giving* (Nashville, TN: Abingdon Press, 1983, 2001).

19 Kavanagh, p. 45.

20 Ibid., pp. 94–5.

21 Long, p. 13. See Paul Westermeyer, *The Church Musician* (Minneapolis, MN: Augsburg, 1997), for an insightful examination of the role of the parish musician or 'cantor'.

22 Long, p. 53.

23 See Robert Hovda, *Strong, Loving and Wise: Presiding in Liturgy* (Washington, DC: Liturgical Conference, 1976).

24 Ibid., p. 14.

25 Electronic communication from then Archbishop Thomas O. Morgan to Richard Leggett, 25 February 2003.

7

THE LITURGICAL FORMATION OF CHILDREN, TEENS, AND YOUNG ADULTS

Ruth A. Meyers

Children and teens in the liturgical assembly

The biography of an American bishop from the early twentieth century describes a whispered conversation in a pew at the time of communion. A young mother had her infant child with her, and she wanted very much to go forward to receive communion. But she could not leave her child in the pew, and she was not sure whether the child would be welcome at the altar rail. The friend sitting with her assured her that the bishop presiding at this liturgy would not be troubled by the appearance of an infant in its mother's arms. 'Are you sure?' asked the young mother. 'Yes. The bishop is quite a nice man. He won't mind,' came the reply. So, with some fear and trembling, the young woman went forward. She was much relieved to find that she was welcome at the rail; the bishop administered communion to her, and no one questioned the presence of her baby.

I am struck by what this story tells us about the experience of children in worship in the Episcopal Church nearly a century ago. The bishop was apparently unlike many other clergy in his willingness to accept the presence of young children in worship, even in a mother's arms at the altar rail. It seems that it was uncommon for young children to be at worship, and certainly unusual for them to come to the altar rail.

Much has changed since that young mother dared to come to the altar rail carrying a baby in her arms. In the United States, a religious education movement flourished in the decades following World War Two. With it came family services, an opportunity for entire families to worship together, whether at Morning Prayer or at Holy Communion, as part of parish education on Sunday morning. Children began to come to the altar rail for a blessing, then started to ask why they couldn't receive communion.[1] A few parishes and dioceses experimented with so-called 'early' admission to communion. There was sufficient momentum that by 1970, the General Convention of the Episcopal Church approved the practice of admitting children to communion before confirmation. Debate continued for many years as to whether infants could be communicated beginning at the time of their baptism, but gradually the practice of communion of all the baptized, including infants, has become widely accepted in the Episcopal Church.[2] The International Anglican Liturgical Consultations at Boston in 1985 and at Toronto in 1991 affirmed this practice, which had also developed in several other provinces of the Anglican Communion.[3]

It might seem, then, that the revisions that came in the wake of the liturgical movement have secured the place of children in the assembly. Unfortunately, this is not so in many parishes in the Episcopal Church. Gretchen Wolff Pritchard, a leading Christian educator, describes the situation this way:

The nurture of children within the parish is commonly known as 'Christian education,' and takes place almost exclusively through a parish structure known as the 'Sunday school,' which models itself on regular school. It is organized in *classes*, with *teachers*, who use *curriculums*, with *lesson plans*. It operates on the unspoken assumption that children must learn how to be Christians, in an academic setting, before they can actually begin to do any of the things that Christians normally do together in the community of faith: pray together, celebrate the sacraments, share their faith and their lives, cherish the hope of things unseen, and bear witness in love and service in the world. And in Episcopal churches, the usual time for Sunday school is *during* the time of the main worship service. Adults come to church on Sunday in order to worship; children come to Sunday school to acquire information.[4]

I have seen several variations on this pattern. In some congregations, children are in Sunday school for the entire duration of the principal Sunday liturgy, perhaps gathering separately for 'children's chapel'. Sometimes parents slip out of the service in order to bring their children in to receive communion. Elsewhere, children spend the liturgy of the Word in their classrooms, the theory being that Christian education is equivalent to the liturgy of the Word, but presented at an age-appropriate level. In this model, children enter the liturgy during the Peace; in some places, there is a formal procession or entrance hymn for the children, calling attention to their arrival in the middle of the liturgy.

As they grow older, this pattern shifts, and children begin to be invited into the assembly. In many parishes, this happens first during elementary school as children are recruited to serve as acolytes. Yet rarely do children become regular members of the worshipping community. Sunday school continues through elementary or junior high school, that is, up to age 11–14, and then a youth group may be provided for teenagers. The youth group typically meets at a time other than Sunday morning, and very few teens have the inclination to come to worship on Sunday mornings, unless their parents insist. Most parents, whatever their expectations of their teenagers for participation in worship, say that it is a battle to get their teenager to church.

The shift then, is not one of fuller participation as a child matures, but of a different reason for minimal or non-participation.

From adults deciding to put children in a classroom instead of the liturgical assembly, the children, as they become teenagers, decide that Sunday worship is not for them. Perhaps they've learned their Sunday school lessons only too well.

The nature of the liturgical assembly

Certainly if we do not include our children fully in worship, we communicate to them that they do not have a place in the assembly. But I think we need to look more closely at how we worship and what that means for the participation of children. Why is it that we think it necessary to keep children away, except perhaps for communion?

Consider the typical pattern of Sunday worship, at least in the Episcopal Church. We value decency and good order. In planning worship, we tend to focus on the sequence of texts interspersed with service music and hymns. Worshippers remain in their place, usually a fixed pew, except for the exchange of the peace and the procession to communion. Although ritual action is part of our worship, including individual movements of sitting, standing, and kneeling, this action tends to be deliberate and staid. Overall, our worship engages the intellect far more than the senses or the emotions.

Consequently, our worship is largely an adult experience, designed by adults and for adults. We expect people who participate to conform, to stay in their place, to adopt the same posture as the rest of the congregation, to speak or sing their lines at the proper times for congregational participation, to listen attentively during the sermon (or at least appear to be doing so). If we allow children to participate, whether as acolytes, or perhaps as members of a children's choir, or simply in the pews with their parents, they are expected to behave, that is, to follow the adult rules. Children who attempt to move about, or are restless, or whisper too loudly at the wrong time, are likely to be admonished by their parents and to receive harsh glares from other worshippers.

In such circumstances, it seems kind to keep children away. 'They're not ready for worship; they're too young,' we tell ourselves. 'Better to keep them in Sunday school, where we can design activities at their own level. When they're older, they'll be able to understand the worship, and then they can participate.'

Such an approach suggests that the problem lies with the children, who are unable to engage worship properly. But perhaps the problem lies with our worship and the way it fails to engage children properly, in the ways they experience the world.

I am not suggesting that we 'water down' our worship, whether by eliminating some portions of the liturgy, or by simplifying the language, or by using children's songs. Each of these may be suitable on occasion, but they tinker primarily with the intellectual dimension of worship and so do not address the broader questions of how worship engages children.

Nor am I suggesting the use of a children's homily. Typically such endeavors invite the children to gather round the preacher at the front of the congregation, where they become a source of amusement for adults. Whether the children's homily takes the form of leading questions addressed to the children or a simple story or the presentation of a concept, the content is primarily cognitive, and frequently it tends towards a moralism that emphasizes doing the right thing. Far more effective than a children's homily is the use of stories as part of the sermon. When my son was younger, our Sunday dinner-table conversations often included discussion of the sermon preached earlier that day. Usually he remembered any stories that were told, whether or not those stories were related to the main point of the homily.

Rather than a children's homily or simplified texts, let us consider a place where we have begun to include children: the communion table. Here, children are engaged not primarily through cognitive understanding, but through experience, the experience of movement to altar rail or communion station, the experience of eating and drinking with other Christians. I suggest that we must consider the entire experience of the liturgy, from gathering

through dismissal, and ask ourselves how children can participate actively with adults throughout the liturgy.

Perhaps we can push this a bit further and ask what children
might have to offer adults through participation in liturgy. After
all, Jesus not only welcomed little children, he told those who
protested the presence of the children:

> Let the little children come to me; do not stop them; for it is
> to such as these that the kingdom of God belongs. Truly I tell
> you, whoever does not receive the kingdom of God as a little
> child will never enter it. (Mark 10.14–15, NRSV)

A few years ago, in an address at a conference on Anglican
worship, David Holeton identified several characteristics of children that might make them exemplary citizens of the reign of
God. Children manifest 'complete and unmitigated trust', the
sort of trust Jesus asks us to place in God. Children are natural and gracious receivers, able to accept, among other things,
the awesome gift of God's grace eagerly, without protestation
or embarrassment. Very young children are helpless to assure
their own survival, surely an image of all people's ultimate dependence on the grace and mercy of God. Children also have
a great capacity for mirth and wonderment.[5] To consider how
these and other qualities of children might affect their participation in worship and their liturgical formation, I turn to studies
of faith development.

Faith development and liturgical formation from infancy to adolescence

Studies of human development by such thinkers as Jean Piaget,
Erik Erikson, and Lawrence Kohlberg offer insight into ways in
which children interact with their environment at various ages,
the developmental tasks they are accomplishing at various stages
of life, and the different ways in which they learn. Drawing upon
these studies and his own in-depth interviews of people of all

ages, four to eighty-four, James Fowler developed a theory of faith development. He explains:

> I believe faith is a human universal. We are endowed at birth with nascent capacities for faith. How these capacities are activated and grow depends to a large extent on how we are welcomed into the world and what kinds of environments we grow in. Faith is interactive and social; it requires community, language, *ritual* and nurture. Faith is also shaped by initiatives from beyond us and other people, initiatives of spirit or grace.[6]

An exploration of these stages of human development and faith development can help us consider how liturgy forms children and how we can form children for participation in liturgy.

At the earliest stage, the first year of life, an infant develops a basic sense of trust or mistrust through interaction with parents and other caregivers who meet the infant's basic needs, including the need for love. Educators David Ng and Virginia Thomas comment, 'When one considers how much of religious life is founded upon trust, one can appreciate the significance of developing in the first year of life a basic sense of trust.'[7] At this stage, liturgical formation consists primarily of the presence of the child at worship. But even in the first year of life, a child interacts with the environment. Infants may be transfixed by light streaming through stained-glass windows, or they may respond to music or babble as they hear others speaking. My hunch is that being in a worshipping community on a regular basis develops a familiarity with sights and sounds that enables a growing child to sense worship as familiar and so as a place and event where she belongs. Giving an infant communion is yet another aspect of participation in the liturgical assembly. Moreover, having infants present and receiving baptism and Eucharist reminds adults that none of us earn God's favour, but rather all of us are dependent upon God's loving kindness.

Carlisle is one child who has been present for worship since she was just a few months old. Her mother began her studies at

Seabury-Western Theological Seminary, where I taught, when Carlisle was about ten months old. Over the course of the three years that her mother attended seminary, I watched Carlisle participate in worship as she grew. For much of the first year, she was simply present with her family at a weekly Eucharist. Usually she would extend her hands eagerly when she came forward with her mother or father to receive communion. As she grew older, I marvelled at her sense of ease in worship and her energy and enthusiasm for liturgy. Although occasionally she became testy and a parent took her out of the assembly for a break, most of the time she was content to be present, sometimes colouring or reading a book, sometimes participating more directly. On occasion, her 'Amen' to the eucharistic prayer could be heard distinctly above the sound of the assembly, showing us what enthusiastic participation can be. In her mother's final year of seminary, the symbols—bread, wine, water—attracted Carlisle more and more. She began to reach up to the font to get some of the holy water in it, sometimes crossing herself after she dipped her hand into the water. When it came time for communion, I would hear her behind me, asking her mother when it would be her turn. Her eagerness renewed my appreciation for the sacraments.

Carlisle had moved into the stage that Fowler calls 'intuitive-projective faith', which extends from ages 2 through 6. The development of language enables the child to begin to make meaning, that is, to name objects and 'organize . . . sensory experience into meaning units'.[8] At this stage the child does not understand cause-and-effect relations, nor can the child reliably generate or retell narrative. However, imagination emerges, unrestrained by logical thought. Images and stories are key to faith formation at this stage. Here the work of Sofia Cavalletti is insightful.

Cavalletti, an Italian scholar of Hebrew, developed a model of catechesis suitable for children ages 3 through 12. Known as the Catechesis of the Good Shepherd, Cavelletti's method draws upon the work of Maria Montessori. Cavalletti developed her methods of religious formation through work with children, first middle-class children in Rome, but then in countries elsewhere in

Europe as well as Africa, Asia, Australia, and North and South America, with urban, rural, and nomadic communities at various socio-economic levels.

At the stage of development corresponding to Fowler's stage of intuitive-projective faith (that is, ages 3 through 6), Cavalletti, like Fowler and others, has found that children intuitively recognize the reality of God and are attracted to God. Their responses to God are characterized by joy and peace. Cavalletti offers this example of a three-year-old girl who had no religious formation; she did not go to nursery school, nor did the family go to church or speak of God:

> One day [the girl] questioned her father about the origin of the world: 'where does the world come from?' Her father replied, in a manner consistent with his ideas, with a discourse that was materialistic in nature; then he added; 'However, there are those who say that all this comes from a very powerful being, and they call him God.' At this point the little girl began to run like a whirlwind around the room in a burst of joy, and exclaimed: 'I knew what you told me wasn't true; it is Him, it is Him!'[9]

Cavalletti explains that at this stage, children's experience of God is not sustained for long periods of time but occurs in 'ephemeral moments, like a flash of light that shines vibrantly and then fades away'.[10] For children at worship during this stage, we can expect that they may have moments at which they are aware of God's presence, even though they cannot follow the logical sequence of the liturgy. Perhaps parents and friends can assist them by quietly calling attention to images, symbols, and actions in the liturgy.

I did this for my four-year-old grandson several years ago. At that time his parents were not taking him to church, and he had little experience of the liturgy. During the eucharistic prayer, I encouraged him to watch the priest's actions, pointing them out as the prayer continued. At the words over the cup, 'This is my blood of the new covenant,' he turned to me and said, 'You mean that stuff is Jesus's blood? Cool!' I was struck by the ease with which he was able to accept the reality of the symbol, that is, the real presence of Christ in the Eucharist; he didn't need explanations that many adults would seek.

This experience with my grandson underscored for me the extent to which young children have religious insight. Sofia Cavalletti's catechetical method creates an environment in which children are able to encounter and experience the mystery of God. As her title 'Catechesis of the Good Shepherd' suggests, the Johannine parable of the good shepherd is central to the method. A catechist presents scripture to the children, reading a selected parable and using small wooden figures to provide a visual and tactile experience of the story. The children respond, first by discussion with the catechist, then through individual activities in their atrium, as the classroom is called. Some may re-enact the parable, using the wooden figures; others might draw or work with different materials.

Formation for liturgy is one aspect of the catechesis. The catechist tells the children that the Good Shepherd is present in the bread and wine; for this presentation the sheep used for the parable are now placed around a small altar. Subsequent presentations about the Eucharist, using small models of a chalice and paten, emphasize 'gift', God's gift as exemplified in the epiclesis and accompanying gesture, our gift as represented by the elevation during the doxology at the conclusion of the eucharistic prayer. Cavalletti explains: 'The children find in these gestures a reference point that acts as an immediate aid to their conscious participation in the celebration.'[11] Learning the names of eucharistic vessels also facilitates participation: 'Numerous mothers remark that as their children come to know these things their attitude to Mass changes. Church is no longer a place where everything is unknown to them; now they see objects that are familiar.'[12]

The Catechesis of the Good Shepherd offers us one example of liturgical formation that enables young children to participate in liturgy more consciously and fully. This method is effective because it engages children in a manner suitable to their developmental stage. Sensory experience is important. Images, stories, and symbols are presented but not explained. Catechists invite the children to ponder what is presented instead of asking children to give the 'right' answer. Always, the catechists expect God to be at work in their midst, and they are trained to listen with the children for God's initiative.

As children reach age six, they move into a new developmental stage. Piaget calls this, from a cognitive perspective, 'concrete operations'. Children begin to perceive reality in a more orderly and systematic fashion. They can follow the logic of a narrative and retell it in great detail. As in the earlier stage, these children think concretely and literally, although now they are able to consider perspectives other than their own.

Fowler calls this stage of faith development 'mythic-literal'. Stories are very important, contributing to the child's sense of identity and belonging to the community. The child is not yet able to step back and formulate concepts, but the narratives gives a new sense of coherence to the worldview.[13]

Cavalletti notes both similarities to the previous stage and several important developments:

> Like the younger child, the older child has the capacity to grasp the Mystery in its essentiality and to move within the world of Mystery with ease and spontaneity . . . The response of the older child differs from that of the younger child as to its rhythm: The pace quickens. Moreover, whereas the younger child returns again and again, without fatigue, to the same subject or theme . . . the older child seeks to expand the horizons of the theme.[14]

For children at this stage, Cavalletti's method focuses on covenant. Because these children are now able to construct and retell narratives, they explore salvation history, from creation to parousia.

Formation for liturgy continues to be one aspect of the catechesis. Cavalletti encourages children to connect the Eucharist to salvation history. She illustrates the development of children's perspective, from the self-referential view of young children to the broader outlook that emerges in this later stage:

> Four-and-a-half-year-old Rachel (from Chicago, Illinois) perceived that the gift is . . . personal. When her catechist was presenting the gesture of epiclesis and was repeating the words from the Episcopal rite: 'Sanctify these gifts [by] your Holy Spirit [to be] for your people . . .' Rachel piped in: 'and for Rachel.' A seven-year-old boy (from College Station, Texas) saw the hands poised in the gesture of epiclesis as the hands of God extended over the world . . . [N]ine-year-old Juan (from Buenos Aires, Argentina) links the epiclesis gesture to the history of salvation he has been learning about. He sees that the gift God sends is directed toward the fulfillment of the history, the parousia.[15]

Learning and reflecting on the memorial acclamation – 'Christ has died, Christ is risen, Christ will come again' – helps these children develop a rudimentary understanding of the paschal mystery. They are not able to think abstractly about this concept, but they know the reality of life and death, growth and transformation, and they are able to connect the memorial acclamation with the biblical stories of Jesus's death and resurrection.

Because these older children can now think sequentially, they learn and follow the sequence of the liturgy. I still remember my excitement – and my sense of pride – when at age 6 I first picked up a prayer book and followed the liturgy from start to finish. My grandson received a Book of Common Prayer when he was baptized at age seven. He was very excited to realize that he could bring the prayer book to church and follow the service.

As children move through this stage, there are many possibilities for them to participate in liturgy. In Erik Erikson's developmental model, children aged 6–12 are developing a sense of 'industry', that is, they learn to use their physical and intellectual capacities to contribute productively to group activities. It is important to think creatively and expansively about how children can contribute to worship beyond following along throughout the liturgy, beyond being acolytes, beyond participating in a children's choir. I have seen children at this stage serve as greeters, welcoming people to the liturgy; help take up the collection; bake the eucharistic bread as well as presenting it at the preparation of the table. By age ten, some children are able to read scripture publicly and lead the intercessions. In one congregation I visited, two ten-year-old girls came to me after the liturgy and invited me to watch as they went about doing the work of the altar guild. They explained proudly that they could do everything, except that an adult had to supervise when they handled the wine.

Involving children in these ways enables them to develop a sense of competence as well as seeing themselves as part of the worshipping community. It also shapes their identity as Christians who are members of a particular parish. If the liturgy is shaping a community that understands itself to be called to acts of justice and compassion, children will also be formed to do justice and love kindness.

As they move into adolescence, critical transitions begin. Abstract thinking becomes possible. As their thinking becomes increasingly flexible and complex, adolescents develop the ability to step aside from narrative and to form and test theories. They are able to reflect about themselves and their lives, and the task of identity formation becomes primary. Peer relationships become particularly important, along with those of family, school, work, and religion.

Fowler characterizes faith development at this stage as 'synthetic-conventional'. Faith can provide a coherent orientation as life becomes increasingly complex. Interpersonal relationships are the principal context for faith formation; adolescents are acutely sensitive to the experience and judgements of significant others, peers as well as adults.[16]

The development of abstract thinking means that adolescents are able to reflect on the symbols and rituals they experience. Formation for liturgy, then, can include opportunity for them to ponder the significance of their experiences, to talk about what happens in liturgy and what it means.

The Sunday liturgy can continue to be important, and as their capacities increase, adolescents are able to handle even more responsibility for liturgical ministries. I think that we often do not give our teenagers significant credit for their abilities. For example, the canons of the Episcopal Church require one to be licensed by the bishop in order to be a eucharistic minister, and until 2003 the canons also stipulated that to be licensed one must be a confirmed adult communicant in good standing, adult defined as age 16 or older.[17] Yet I have seen youth as young as 11–12 assist in distributing communion quite ably, with every bit of reverence and sense of presence I would expect of an adult. What barriers do we place that keep our youth from offering themselves to the full extent of their abilities? In Jewish tradition, children at a Bar or Bat Mitzvah, marking a transition to adult faith at age 13, not only read scripture, they also preach, giving *Devar Torah*, that is, a 'word of Torah'.[18] Do we ever in Christian tradition allow adolescents to preach, that is, to interpret Scripture publicly, in the midst of the Sunday assembly? Do we provide formation that enables them to join in the proclamation of the word? How might adolescents lead adults into new understandings, if we authorize them to speak in the liturgical assembly on occasion?

I mentioned earlier that most parents speak despairingly of their struggles to get their teenagers to the Sunday assembly. I suspect that this is not simply about worship but rather expresses the teens' uncertainty about whether they belong at all in the church. In what ways do they participate in the community of faith? Are their perspectives heard and respected? Do they have opportunities to help plan and prepare for the assembly's liturgy?

Along with the intergenerational context of Sunday worship, opportunities to worship primarily with peers can be particularly significant during adolescence. After all, peer interaction is critical to the identity formation that occurs at this stage. I have seen teenagers who are thoroughly disaffected with the Sunday liturgy become actively engaged when they participate in youth programmes that include worship. For example, in Happening, a teenage renewal movement that has adapted the model of Cursillo, worship is one aspect of the formation of Christian community. During a Happening weekend, teens reflect on their life experience in small groups, some give talks in which they witness to God's work in their lives, and together they worship, pray, sing, eat, and play intensively. Worship engages them fully. I asked my son at age 18 to explain why worship 'worked' for him at Happening but not in the parish on Sunday morning. He responded, 'You can sing and do crazy things [by this he means clapping, foot stomping, and occasional shouts during songs]. The service isn't as long; well, I don't know time-wise if it's any shorter, but it seems shorter. It's not boring.' In this context, liturgy helps form a community, and the formation of community enables worship to be richly participatory.

I have not yet mentioned confirmation because I do not think it should be the primary emphasis in liturgical formation (or, more broadly, Christian formation) with adolescents. Certainly the affirmation of faith made at confirmation can be significant in adolescent identity formation, and preparation for confirmation can provide a context in which adolescents can explore the meaning of liturgy as well as other aspects of Christian faith and life. But baptism is full initiation, at whatever age it is celebrated. Affirmation of baptismal faith and commitment to the responsibilities of baptism are expressed in many ways throughout Christian life. This affirmation and commitment should already be occurring from the time of early childhood. Undue emphasis on a particular moment of affirmation can diminish the importance of ongoing Christian commitment.

Liturgical formation and young adults

In the Episcopal Church, there is growing concern about the low participation of people aged 18–35. A 2008 survey found that Episcopalians tend to be significantly older than the general US population, with a majority (62%) of Episcopal congregations reporting that more than half of their members are over age 50.

Young adults aged 18–34 comprise about 23% of the U.S. population, but only 12% of Episcopalians are in this age range.[19] Those young adults who do come often have not been raised in the Episcopal Church.

In the United States, dropping out of church as a young adult is common, not just in the Episcopal Church but more broadly across denominations. One study found that over 60% of young adults leave church for two years or more. While there is evidence of a pattern of dropping out in young adulthood for at least the past century, the average age at which this occurs has dropped, from age 29 in the middle of the twentieth century to age 18 by the early 1990s.[20]

Some of the dropout might be attributed to ineffective formation of children and teens, or an all-too-effective message of exclusion communicated as children grow up in the church. But I think there is more here. The identity formation experienced so intensely in adolescence continues for young adults, at least those in the United States. The phenomenon of church dropouts might reflect, at least in part, faith development during young adulthood.

Sharon Daloz Parks, a researcher who has been both a college chaplain and a university professor, proposes that young adulthood is not so much an extended adolescence as it is a distinctive period of development in which the young person, standing at the threshold of adulthood, grapples with questions of commitment, vocation, and social role and lifestyle. Parks has found that young adults are seeking both an ideal, or a dream, and a community to ground them. While there is great promise, there is also a great vulnerability as young adult faith develops.[21]

What might it mean for liturgy and liturgical formation were we to recognize that young adults are in a critical stage of faith formation? Parks suggests, 'People and institutions who hope to serve as an anchoring authority for young adults must offer a vision of self, world, and "God" that resonates with the experience and critical capacity of young adults themselves.'[22] The quality often suggested in the United States is authenticity. I think that this means consistency between belief and action, that is, that our practices embody what we profess. Our liturgy must acknowledge the reality of our human struggles and sinfulness, as well as our hopes and triumphs, and it must enable the transformation of the people of God.

Because identity formation includes coming to understand the reasons for one's actions and assessing the consistency of beliefs, values, emotions, and actions, formation for liturgy with young adults might be most effective by providing opportunity for young adults to reflect with other adults on why we worship as we do and the significance of worship for Christian faith and life. This would be especially significant for those who are new to the Episcopal Church and Anglicanism, but I have found that many young adults who were raised in the church are ready, perhaps for the first time in their lives, for a more in-depth exploration of the meaning of liturgy. Of course, for this formation to be most effective, it is important that there be some coherence between the liturgical expressions of the faith community and congregational life.

Participation in the creative work of planning and preparing for liturgy is also important for young adults. Just as we might learn from young children how to be trusting and receptive to God, so young adults might teach those of us who are no longer quite so young new ways for liturgy to be a vital expression of Christian faith and a transformative encounter with the God of Jesus Christ.

Conclusion

The Catechism of the Book of Common Prayer 1662 (and that of previous prayer books) teaches that in baptism a child 'was made a member of Christ, the child of God, and inheritor of the kingdom of heaven'. As full members of the Body of Christ, children ought also to be full participants in the worship of that Body. The challenge for congregations is to discover what liturgical practices and experiences of formation will enable children of all ages to engage in liturgy in a manner suited to their developmental capacities. Moreover, by attending to the experience of children, teens, and young adults, congregations might learn from them something about the meaning of liturgy, and all in the liturgical assembly might come to receive the reign of God like little children.

Notes

1 David Holeton, 'Communion of All the Baptized and Anglican Tradition', *Children at the Table: A Collection of Essays on Children and the Eucharist*, ed. Ruth A. Meyers (New York: Church Hymnal Corp., 1995), pp. 33–4.

2 Ruth A. Meyers, *Continuing the Reformation: Re-Visioning Baptism in the Episcopal Church* (New York: Church Publishing Inc., 1997), pp. 93–101, 153–6, 234–6.

3 Colin Buchanan, ed., *Nurturing Children in Communion: Essays from the Boston Consultation*, Grove Liturgical Study 44 (Bramcote, Nottingham: Grove Books, 1985); David R. Holeton, ed., *Christian Initiation in the Anglican Communion: The Toronto Statement 'Walk in Newness of Life'; The Findings of the Fourth International Anglican Liturgical Consultation, Toronto 1991*, Grove Worship Series 118 (Bramcote, Nottingham: Grove Books, 1991).

4 Gretchen Wolff Pritchard, *Offering the Gospel to Children* (Cambridge, MA: Cowley Publications, 1992), pp. 140–1; emphasis in original.

5 David Holeton, 'Welcome Children, Welcome Me', *Anglican Theological Review* 82 (2000): 97–101; address given at 'Unbound! Anglican Worship Beyond the Prayer Book,' conference at Church Divinity School of the Pacific, January 1999.

6 James Fowler, *Stages of Faith: The Psychology of Human Development and the Quest for Meaning* (San Francisco: Harper & Row, 1981), xiii; emphasis added.

7 David Ng and Virginia Thomas, *Children in the Worshiping Community* (Atlanta: John Knox Press, 1981), p. 32.

8 Fowler, *Stages of Faith*, p. 123.

9 Sofia Cavalletti, *The Religious Potential of the Child*, trans. Patricia M. Coulter and Julie M. Coulter (New York: Paulist Press, 1983), p. 32.

10 Ibid., p. 36.

11 Ibid., p. 83.

12 Ibid., p. 91.

13 Fowler, *Stages of Faith*, pp. 149–50.

14 Sofia Cavalletti, *The Religious Potential of the Child 6 to 12 Years Old*, trans. Rebekah Rojcewicz and Alan R. Perry (Chicago: Liturgy Training Publications, 2002), p. x.

15 Ibid., pp. 60–1.

16 Fowler, *Stages of Faith*, pp. 172–3.

17 In 2003, the canons were amended to read 'confirmed communicant in good standing', rather than 'confirmed adult communicant in good standing'.

18 Debra R. Blank, 'Jewish Rites of Adolescence', in *Life Cycles in Jewish and Christian Worship*, Two Liturgical Traditions Vol. 4 ed. Paul Bradshaw and Lawrence Hoffman (Notre Dame, IN: University of Notre Dame Press, 1996), pp. 81–2.

19 'Episcopal Congregations Overview: Findings from the 2008 Faith Communities Today Survey', p. 2; at http://www.episcopalchurch.org/documents/Episcopal_Overview_FACT_2008.pdf; accessed 28 October 2009.

20 Wade Clark Roof, *A Generation of Seekers* (San Francisco: Harper SanFrancisco, 1993), pp. 55; 154–5; 279, n. 2.

21 Sharon Parks, *The Critical Years: The Young Adult Search for a Faith to Live By* (San Francisco: Harper & Row, 1986), pp. 73–106.

22 Ibid., pp. 99–100.

Appendix
Short History of the International Anglican Liturgical Consultation

Cynthia Botha

The International Anglican Liturgical Consultation (IALC) owes its existence to the passion and concerns of a small group of academic liturgists committed to the ecumenical study of liturgy, in particular its expression in the Anglican Communion. Meeting together at the Congress of *Societas Liturgica* (an international and ecumenical society of academic liturgists) in 1983 in Vienna, they identified the need to meet regularly to consider liturgical matters pertaining to the Anglican Communion. After this meeting, David Holeton, with the assistance of Donald Gray from England, started co-ordinating the first IALC, to precede the meeting of *Societas Liturgica* in Boston in 1985. They compiled the first list of persons to be invited, people with whom they had contact and were known to have an interest in matters liturgical.

The nature of changes in the world, especially the moves to independence of many of the commonwealth countries that were formerly members of the British Empire, has required the Anglican Communion to face new challenges in its thinking and practice. This is reflected in the nature of the topics covered and statements issued from the meetings of the IALC. It is also reflected in the church politics that lie beneath the IALC's struggle to be recognized.

Before we deal with the eight consultations, we need to understand something of the principles guiding the IALC. From the beginning, the co-ordinators agreed that:

1 A statement would be issued after each consultation.
2 The membership needed to be as widely representative of the Anglican Communion as possible, and funds to enable this would be needed.
3 Consultations would coincide with the *Societas Liturgica* to enable as many liturgists as possible to attend.
4 An 'ecumenical partner' would be invited to each consultation to journey alongside them.

The first consultation took place in Boston in 1985. The members agreed to consider the resolution arising from the 1968 Lambeth Conference concerning the theology of initiation and admission to communion. The issues considered here were:

1 What makes one a member of an Anglican church?
2 Does one need to be confirmed to receive communion?

The 'Boston Statement' issued following that meeting presented the participants' conclusion that baptism is the sole sacrament allowing one to become a full member of the church. It further affirmed that admission to communion is not dependent on confirmation. It called on all provinces to recognize those admitted to communion in other provinces and to review their baptismal rites and their constitution and canons in the light of this statement.

This report had only the status of those making the recommendations, as the IALC was not yet recognized by the Anglican Consultative Council (ACC). The issue of initiation and the role of baptism would retain its importance, returning again for further discussion at the fourth consultation, held in Toronto in 1991.

Liturgical formation and education was to have been the theme of the second consultation, in Brixen, Italy, in August 1987. The consultation instead spent most of the plenary time discussing the constitutional position and role of the IALC within the Anglican Communion, in response to Resolution 12 adopted by the ACC at its April 1987 meeting. The ACC had proposed the creation of an Anglican Communion Liturgical Commission, which seemed to undermine the work of the IALC. Resolution 11 of the same ACC meeting had just affirmed the IALC as being worthy of support! The 'Brixen Submission', sent to the Anglican Communion office opposing the idea of a 'commission', recommended instead a 'consultation'. No statement was issued from the IALC meeting, and the intended topic of 1987 was next considered at the 2003 consultation.

The third consultation was held in York in 1989 and explored the topic of 'liturgical inculturation'. Already in 1987, through Uganda, Africa had challenged what was regarded as western cultural imperialism with regard to Anglican liturgy in Africa. The 1989 consultation took seriously this input and made provision for delegates from Ghana, Nigeria, and Sri Lanka to attend. As a result a major statement was issued: 'Down to Earth Worship'. This outlined principles of liturgical inculturation and offered examples. It remains a 'major signpost for Anglican liturgical development'.[1]

Post 1987 and before the 1989 consultation, the Lambeth Conference had met. There was suspicion among some members as to what the liturgists were doing and a desire to control them, and a motion was put forward which liturgists correctly saw amounted to 'policing' their work. This was not acted upon by the primates subsequently, and in 1993 the motion was finally laid to rest. The primates did appoint a bishop to attend IALC and serve on its steering committee, and thereby maintained a link with the body.

Also, on a more positive note, further recommendations were made for the Standing Committee of the ACC to find ways of working with the IALC. A constructive informal meeting was held with some ACC and IALC members, and the idea of a liturgical commission was shelved. This official recognition was very encouraging to the IALC and as a result, the 1989 consultation prepared the guidelines by which the IALC would operate in the future.

The fourth consultation, held in Toronto in 1991, made two important decisions:

1 At this gathering the African members caucused for a consultation in Africa, which took place in 1993 in Kanamai (near Mombasa), Kenya, and further considered the topic of inculturation.[2]

2 After the Toronto gathering, the Steering Committee, seeking to ensure the fullest representation of the Anglican Communion and realizing that funding was to continue to be a problem, decided that full consultations would only be held every four years. This would allow for every effort to be made to have as wide a representation as possible. It was agreed that preparatory conferences would be held in the intervening two-year period.

An important development at this time was the appointment of the Revd Paul Gibson as Co-ordinator for Liturgy for the ACC. He was seconded by the Anglican Church of Canada. This appointment strengthened the link with the ACC, as Paul Gibson was to play an increasing role in the administration of IALC and become its public face.

The Eucharist assumed prominence at the fifth consultation, at Dublin in 1995. Its 'Principles and Recommendations' remain insightful and thought-provoking some fourteen years later. It began to tackle the relationship between the role of the laity and the ordained in liturgy and looked at the future role of leaders in the church, whom it suggested should be 'open to renewal and able to facilitate and enable it in community'.[3]

The work on the Eucharist began with a preparatory conference held at Untermarchtal, Germany, in August 1993. The next preparatory conference, held in Järvenpää, Finland, in 1997, considered the subject of ordination. This conference was intended to lead to a full consultation in Kottayam, India, in 1999. The Kottayam consultation, however, did not happen as the Indian authorities banned it just one day before it was scheduled to begin! This was because the conference was not registered with the government and no special visa had been applied for. Participants who had nonetheless been able to travel to India agreed to change the status of the meeting to that of a conference, and work continued on the ordinal.

The work on the ordinal was concluded at the sixth consultation, held in Berkeley, California, in 2001, when a major statement, 'To Equip the Saints', was agreed by the consultation.[4] This statement reaffirmed the place of baptism as the foundation of life and ministry in the church and that the laying on of hands with prayer is absolutely central to the rite of ordination, while other ceremonies are secondary. The issue of the relationship of orders to particular church structures and that of culture and ministry were also considered. In response to this statement, many provinces have engaged in liturgical revision of their ordinal.

The Berkeley consultation was followed by another preparatory conference, this one held in 2003 in Cuddesdon, Oxford, England. This meeting once again considered the question of liturgical education and formation.

An important issue raised by Paul Gibson at the Berkeley consultation concerned the question of eucharistic food, and the consultation requested the ACC to conduct a survey to determine the practice around the Anglican Communion in relation to the elements of Holy Communion. The meeting in 2003 appointed a small task team to review the results of the survey and report back to the full consultation in 2005. The 2005 consultation endorsed the report and recommendations of this task group.[5]

Since 2003, there have been three further consultations: the seventh, held in Prague in 2005, looked at the question of 'liturgy and Anglican identity',[6] and the eighth, in 2007 in Palermo, Sicily, considered funerals and other rites surrounding death. The ninth consultation, held in Auckland, New Zealand, in

2009, considered the theology, rites, and practice of marriage. This topic was not finalized, nor was the document from 2007 on 'rites surrounding death', and no statement issued.[7] It was agreed that more work was needed.

In his 2000 report on the IALC, Paul Gibson said that the effectiveness of the consultations is dependent on three factors:

1 support from provinces in sending representatives to consultations;
2 commitment from provinces to study and respond to the statements issued; and
3 the initiative from provinces to identify areas of concern for the closer attention of the IALC, including reporting on their own liturgical revision and developments. These reports have become an important part of the meetings.[8]

These three factors retain their importance for us today.

In conclusion, it is encouraging to note how the IALC, through its work, continues to be at the forefront of bringing theology and praxis together. Central to its core belief continues to be the issue first highlighted at its first consultation, namely, the importance of baptism for us as Anglicans as a way of belonging and as the cornerstone of all ministries.

Notes

1 David Holeton and Colin Buchanan, *A History of the International Anglican Liturgical Consultations 1983–2007*, Alcuin/GROW Joint Liturgical Studies 63 (Norwich: SCM-Canterbury Press, 2007), p. 28.

2 David Gitari, ed., *Anglican Liturgical Inculturation in Africa: The Kanamai Statement 'African Culture and Anglican Liturgy'*, Alcuin/GROW Liturgical Study 28 (Bramcote, Nottingham: Grove Books, 1994).

3 David R. Holeton, ed., *Renewing the Anglican Eucharist: Findings of the Fifth International Anglican Liturgical Consultation, Dublin, Eire, 1995*, Grove Worship Series 135 (Cambridge: Grove Books, 1996), p. 7.

4 'The Berkeley Statement: To Equip the Saints' is available online at http://www.anglicancommunion.org/ministry/liturgy/docs/berkeley.pdf.

5 'Eucharistic Food and Drink: A report of the Inter-Anglican Liturgical Commission [sic] to the Anglican Consultative Council', http://www.anglicancommunion.org/ministry/liturgy/docs/ialcreport.cfm#_ftn1, accessed 4/10/09.

6 The 2005 statement on 'Liturgy and Anglican Identity' is available online at http://www.anglicancommunion.org/ministry/liturgy/docs/ialc2005statement.cfm.

7 A communiqué summarizes the work of the 2009 meeting: http://www.anglicancommunion.org/ministry/liturgy/docs/ialc2009communique.cfm.

8 Paul Gibson, 'International Anglican Liturgical Consultations: A Review', http://www.anglicancommunion.org/ministry/liturgy/docs/ialcreview.cfm, accessed 4/10/09.

Acknowledgements

David Holeton and Colin Buchanan, *A History of the International Anglican Liturgical Consultations 1983–2007*, Joint Liturgical Studies 63 (Norwich: SCM-Canterbury Press, 2007).

Paul Gibson, 'International Anglican Liturgical Consultations: A Review.' September 2000. http://www.anglicancommunion.org/ministry/liturgy/docs/ialcreview.cfm

Publications: The Work of the International Anglican Liturgical Consultation

Buchanan, Colin, ed., *Nurturing Children in Communion: Essays from the Boston Consultation*, Grove Liturgical Study 44 (Nottingham: Grove Books, 1985).

Meyers, Ruth A., ed., *Children at the Table: The Communion of All the Baptized in Anglicanism Today* (New York: Church Hymnal Corporation, 1995). Includes the findings from the 1985 Boston meeting; essays from the Boston consultation, including 3 not published in the Grove Liturgical Study; and 3 additional essays.

Talley, Thomas J., ed., *A Kingdom of Priests: Liturgical Formation of the People of God; Papers read at the International Anglican Liturgical Consultation, Brixen, North Italy, 24–25 August 1987*, Alcuin/GROW Liturgical Study 5 (Nottingham: Grove Books, 1988).

Holeton, David R., ed., *Liturgical Inculturation in the Anglican Communion, including the York Statement 'Down to Earth Worship'*, Alcuin/GROW Liturgical Study 15 (Nottingham: Grove Books, 1990).

Holeton, David R., ed., *Christian Initiation in the Anglican Communion: The Toronto Statement 'Walk in Newness of Life'; The Findings of the Fourth International Anglican Liturgical Consultation, Toronto 1991*, Grove Worship Series 118 (Nottingham: Grove Books, 1991).

Holeton, David R., ed., *Growing in Newness of Life: Christian Initiation in Anglicanism Today; Papers from the Fourth International Anglican Liturgical Consultation, Toronto 1991* (Toronto, Ontario: Anglican Book Centre, 1993).

Holeton, David R., ed., *Revising the Eucharist: Groundwork for the Anglican Communion; Studies in Preparation for the 1995 Dublin Consultation*, Alcuin/GROW Liturgical Study 27 (Nottingham: Grove Books, 1994).

Holeton, David R., ed., *Renewing the Anglican Eucharist: Findings of the Fifth International Anglican Liturgical Consultation, Dublin, Eire, 1995*, Grove Worship Series 135 (Cambridge: Grove Books, 1996).

Holeton, David R., ed., *Our Thanks and Praise: The Eucharist in Anglicanism Today; Papers from the Fifth International Anglican Liturgical Consultation* (Toronto, Ontario: Anglican Book Centre, 1998).

Holeton, David R., ed., *Anglican Orders and Ordinations: Essays and Reports from the Interim Conference at Jarvenpää, Finland, of the International Anglican Liturgical Consultation, 4–9 August 1997*, Joint Liturgical Studies 39 (Cambridge: Grove Books, 1997).

Gibson, Paul, ed., *Anglican Ordination Rites: The Berkeley Statement 'To Equip the Saints'; Findings of the Sixth International Anglican Liturgical Consultation, Berkeley, California, 2001*, Grove Worship Series 168 (Cambridge: Grove Books, 2002).

Dowling, Ronald L. and David R. Holeton, eds, *Equipping the Saints: Ordination in Anglicanism Today; Papers from the Sixth International Anglican Liturgical Consultation* (Blackrock, Co. Dublin: Columba Press, 2006).

Irvine, Christopher, ed., *Anglican Liturgical Identity; Papers from the Prague meeting of the International Anglican Liturgical Consultation*, Joint Liturgical Studies 65 (Norwich: SCM-Canterbury Press, 2008).

FOR FURTHER READING

Anderson, Herbert and Edward Foley, *Mighty Stories, Dangerous Rituals: Weaving Together the Human and the Divine* (San Francisco: Jossey Bass, 1998).

Bartlett, Alan, David Stancliffe, John Thompson, and Lizette Larson Miller, *Renewing the Eucharist: Table* (Norwich: Canterbury Press, 2009).

Bell, John, *The Singing Thing: A Case for Congregational Song* (Chicago: GIA Publications, 2000).

Bradshaw, Paul and Peter Moger, eds., *Worship Changes Lives: How it Works, Why it Matters* (London: Church House Publishing, 2008).

Dawtry, Anne, and Christopher Irvine, *Art and Worship*, Alcuin Liturgy Guides 2 (London: SPCK, 2002).

Duck, Ruth C., *Finding Words for Worship: A Guide for Leaders* (Louisville, KY: Westminster John Knox Press, 1995).

Earey, Mark, *Liturgical Worship: A Fresh Look – How it Works; Why it Matters* (London: Church House Publishing, 2002).

Earey, Mark, *Worship as Drama*, Grove Worship Series 140 (Cambridge: Grove Books, 1997).

Fairless, Caroline, *Children at Worship: Congregations in Bloom* (New York: Church Publishing, 2000).

Gelineau, Joseph, *The Liturgy Today and Tomorrow* (London: Darton, Longman, and Todd, 1978).

Gibson, Paul, *Patterns of Celebration: Layers of Meaning in the Structure of the Eucharist* (Toronto: Anglican Book Centre, 1998).

Giles, Richard, Mark Ireland, Ann Loades and Nicola M. Slee, *Renewing the Eucharist: Journey* (Norwich: Canterbury Press, 2008).

Gregory, Andrew, Gordon Mursell, Jo Bailey and Joy Tetley, *Renewing the Eucharist: Word* (Norwich: Canterbury Press, 2009).

Guiver, George, *Pursuing the Mystery* (London: SPCK, 1996).

Irvine, Christopher, *The Art of God: The Making of Christians and the Meaning of Worship* (London: SPCK / Chicago: Liturgy Training Publications, 2005).

Irvine, Christopher, *The Use of Symbols in Worship*, Alcuin Liturgy Guides 4 (London: SPCK, 2007).

Lee, Jeffrey, *Opening the Prayer Book*, The New Church's Teaching Series, Vol. 7 (Cambridge, MA: Cowley Publications, 1999).

McCall, Richard D., *Do This: Liturgy as Performance* (Notre Dame, IN: University of Notre Dame Press, 2007).

Morris, Clayton L., *Holy Hospitality: Worship and the Baptismal Covenant* (New York: Church Publishing, Inc., 2005).

Pearson, Sharon Ely, and Robyn Szoke, eds, *The Prayer Book Guide to Christian Education*, 3rd edition (Harrisburg, PA/ London: Morehouse Publishing, 2009).

Smith, George Wayne, *Admirable Simplicity: Principles for Worship Planning in the Anglican Tradition* (New York, NY: The Church Hymnal Corporation, 1996).

Stevenson, Kenneth, and Bryan Spinks, eds., *The Identity of Anglican Worship* (Oxford: Mowbray, 1991).

Tammany, Klara, *Living Water: Baptism as a Way of Life* (New York, NY: Church Publishing, 2002).

Vanderwell, Howard, ed., *The Church of All Ages: Generations Worshiping Together* (Herndon, VA: Alban Institute, 2008).

Weil, Louis, *A Theology of Worship*, The New Church's Teaching Series, Vol. 12 (Cambridge, MA: Cowley Publications, 2002).

Westerhoff, John, *Living Faithfully as a Prayer Book People* (Harrisburg, PA/ London: Morehouse Publishing, 2004).

Yust, Karen Marie, *Real Kids, Real Faith* (San Francisco: Jossey Bass, 2004).

INDEX

Canterbury Studies in Anglicanism
Christ and Culture
Edited by Martyn Percy, Mark Chapman, Ian Markham and Barney Hawkins

978 1 85311 987 3   216 x 135mm   160pp   £14.99

In this first volume in an important new series, leading figures from around the Anglican Communion including **Tom Wright, Geoffrey Rowell, Michael Jackson, Ian Douglas** and **Stephen Pickard** reflect on the themes of the 2008 Lambeth conference. These range from Anglican identity, evangelism and living under scripture, to human sexuality, gender violence, the environment and social injustice.

Christ and Culture aims to open up the Lambeth themes to the wider church for grassroots conversation and reflection and to provide a resource for seminaries and theological colleges training the next generation of Anglican leaders.

'We need the kind of exact and imaginative study this series offers us… so that our life in the Communion will be enriched as well as calmed, challenged as well as reinforced.'
- Rowan Williams

Available from all good bookshops
or direct from Canterbury Press
Tel: + 44 (0)1603 612914   www.canterburypress.co.uk

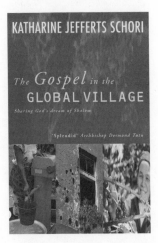